HOW TO MANAGE DESPITE YOUR BOSS

ERWIN HÖHN
& ADI NELL

HOW TO MANAGE DESPITE YOUR BOSS

Matador
9 Priory Business Park,
Wistow Road
Kibworth Beauchamp
Leicester LE8 0RX, UK
Tel: (+44) 116 279 2299
Fax: (+44) 116 279 2277
Email: books@troubador.co.uk
Web: www.troubador.co.uk/matador

ISBN 978 1784621 629

British Library Cataloguing in Publication Data.
A catalogue record for this book is available from the British Library.

Printed and bound by CPI Group (UK) Ltd, Croydon, CR0 4YY
Typeset in 11pt Aldine by Troubador Publishing Ltd, Leicester, UK

Matador is an imprint of Troubador Publishing Ltd

MIX
Paper from
responsible sources
FSC® C013604

CONTENTS

READ THIS FIRST!

You haven't picked up this book by accident. Something in the title grabbed you and made you open it up and read this preface. What was that?

Many managers live a life of frustration. Sure, there are the rewards of seeing your team achieve great things and getting praise for a job well done. But so many of us are held back by the bosses who hired us. So often you have a great idea but he just won't agree. You can save him money, you can make the whole organisation run more smoothly, but he's having none of it. What's even more frustrating is that so many other people at work feel the same way!

We've all experienced great bosses – but they're rare beasts, indeed. Far more common are their insecure little brothers, trying much harder to avoid failure than to achieve greatness. For every great boss there are dozens, possibly hundreds, of worried, fearful, unhappy despots or indecisive jellies, just trying to get through the day. They really don't help you to achieve the results you crave.

Why does this happen? Is he fearful? Why is he so resistant to change? And do you, or the organisation, have what it takes to achieve what you believe is possible?

This book answers these questions, and more. It gives

you a tool kit to work with, explains who (and what) to ask and how to interpret both resistance and support. It takes you on a journey from where you are now to where you want to be, holding your hand and reassuring you along the way.

As you riffle through the pages of the book and decide whether to buy it or not (please do!), have a look at the structure we've laid out for you. We're very aware that not everyone will have the time to read this cover to cover like a novel. That's fine. We've purposely designed it to be read in any number of ways.

USER'S GUIDE:

First, you could use this as some kind of 'Dummies' Guide', simply reading the introductory paragraphs at the start of each chapter. That will give you lots and lots of ideas to work with and help you to form your own plan of action. You could then come back to the book to mine certain chapters in more detail if you like.

An alternative is to use our book as a detailed instruction manual or guidebook. What you're trying to do is a little like visiting a new town; the chapters in our guide lead you to the important and interesting places, without which your journey wouldn't be complete. You could skip stages, just as you skip some sights, but imagine visiting Rome without looking at the Colosseum!

If you are able to devote the time to reading the full text, the rewards will be much greater than the simple skimming described earlier. The detail of what we explain is important, and trying to get great results without using all the tips and tricks available to you could easily end in more frustration. That would be a shame.

Finally, and possibly stretching our guidebook metaphor to breaking point, if you wanted to know all there is to know about the Colosseum, you'd have to buy another guide, or probably set of books, to give you that level of detail. So it is with the book: we give an overview of the relevant literature that supports our process, but don't go into great detail on each book or course. If something does prick your interest, we'd be delighted if you'd go and buy the books we refer to – as would their authors!

We really believe this is a trip you'll enjoy. You may be starting with a sense of frustration and annoyance but we're confident that you'll gain so much from your journey that any early discomfort will soon be replaced by a sense of purpose, achievement and hope.

Shall we begin?

THE FRUSTRATION

THE CRUNCHY BIT:

Your boss is in a position of power over you. To get things done you have to go through him, and he's having none of it. This is a common problem – you're not alone! This chapter outlines common causes for your frustration and explains how we're going to go about addressing the concepts and ideas that you'll need to master in order to succeed, in spite of your boss. You need to understand the boss, evaluate the potential of the organisation as well as your own potential, and understand how to develop and harness the enthusiasm of others to your own ends. We don't give much detail here of how to do these things, but explain the process we'll be following and tell you which chapters will deal with each issue. Have a look at pages 12 and 13 for this.

THOROUGHLY FED UP!

Are you fed up at work? Are you frustrated by your inability to get your ideas taken seriously? Do others fail to see your vision of where your organisation could be? Do you feel as if most of your suggestions are being dismissed as impractical or unworkable? Does the slow rate of change in your organisation irritate you – especially when what needs to be done seems self-evident? Are you tired of being told how unique your organisation is and that the solutions you propose won't work here? Do you feel disempowered? Is the person who seems to be standing in your way the very person who hired or promoted you? Your boss.

If this sounds familiar to you, you're just the person we've written this book for. Rather than jumping into too much theory and concept, we'll be using a fictitious character, Jo, to illustrate many of the scenarios and problems you're likely to encounter (or have already!). Jo will be used to contextualise what we're discussing and make it more practical and relevant. We'll follow her closely through the book, adding the theoretical background that will help you deal with your current frustration more effectively.

Jo is a thirty-two-year-old advertising executive. Eighteen months ago she was hired by Brian, director and senior partner of the SimianSynergy Agency, a well-known (and entirely fictitious) global advertising agency. Jo was thrilled when she was offered the job. She had been working at Dullards for five years, patiently working her way up the ladder from junior to senior account manager. But she had become bored and a bit restless, so when the job came up at SimianSynergy, she jumped at it. As well as a leap in salary, she would be in charge of twenty people. This was going to be her first stab at proper management and she couldn't wait.

Jo recalls her first meeting with Brian:

"It was a sunny day when I went for my interview with Brian. He is a legendary figure in the industry and had built Simian from a small start-up to its current global status. I was excited and a little apprehensive, but, given the fact that they'd approached me to head up a major division, I felt reassured that I had something they were looking for.

"At the meeting, Brian was everything I'd heard: dynamic, engaging, charming and visionary. He wanted me to take over the operations of an important area of Simian's activity and to help to take the business to a new level. I was given authority to run my division and have direct access to Brian's help and support whenever I needed it."

Brian started as a copywriter at SimianSynergy when it was a much smaller, below-the-line agency. He was talented and successful, but soon developed an interest in financial management. His role in finance gradually took him out of copy altogether, and he became the financial director a few years later. His lack of formal accounts training did not seem an impediment to his progress; his intellectual ability allowed him to learn very fast, concentrating on the areas of knowledge he needed at any given time. Partnership quickly followed. A few short months after becoming a partner, Simian lost a major account in the financial downturn and had severe cash flow difficulties. It was still a profitable company, but it needed to restructure quickly in order to avoid insolvency. Brian stepped in ruthlessly, axing jobs, restructuring departments and consolidating accounts. His partners' gratitude was short-lived, however, as they found themselves sidelined and without authority. Brian was left completely in charge of the restructured company. Simian proceeded to go from strength to strength as the economy improved and new accounts followed. Brian moved Simian to an above-the-line enterprise and became a very significant player in the industry. Brian's role was regarded as pivotal.

THE BOSS HAS ALL THE POWER...

Jo has lots of drive and ambition and a clear vision of what SimianSynergy could offer. She took the job because Brian seemed so keen to have her on board. Initially she felt that she and Brian shared a common vision for the development of Simian, but now Brian has become her biggest source of frustration. Not only does he not want to branch out into new areas but he seems unwilling to develop the existing accounts in any way.

Brian has become defensive. He is even, on occasion, intolerant or aggressive and seems to take things personally no matter how carefully Jo puts her concerns or ideas. At other times he seems incapable of reaching a decision or stubbornly defends the *status quo* despite new information being available. He seems so unpredictable.

Some of Brian's senior staff have been similarly frustrating. Jo feels that she's not being listened to or that her ideas are being dismissed without being properly considered. On the other hand, many of her new colleagues seem to like her ideas and see merit in them. There have even been encouraging noises from some of the more senior executives, but they don't seem to have the power (or perhaps the inclination) to change things.

The net result is that Jo feels frustrated and fed up. She also seems to have even less input into the running of the agency than she had in her previous position. So she's started to ask herself how she ended up here after such a promising start. She is even beginning to question whether she should stay at Simian.

Does this sound familiar?

HOW DID THIS HAPPEN?

The details are undoubtedly different in your case, but we're sure that at least one of the following points will resonate with you:

- you joined your company because it seemed so well placed to become a major player;

or

- you joined the company because it was already a major player but, on closer inspection, it seems to have gained its success despite its failings

or

- you were hired for your ideas to improve the problems you'd already identified;

or

- you pushed for the job because you believed in the

changes you could make, and were led to believe that you would be supported in making them.

But you are being prevented from implementing the changes you know will help your company by the very person who hired you! Your boss. Frustrated? You bet! And the excuses or rationalisations you are given always seem to be the same: his (we'll use a male boss, but female bosses can be just as frustrating) greater experience in his "unique" market has proved to him that your ideas are theoretical, impractical, unrealistic, too costly or have failed before. Yes, all your ideas – or at least that's how it feels.

Another of your likely frustrations is the waste of human capital within the organisation. It is quite common to find that you are not the only one who feels like this. While it might be reassuring to know that others have seen the same shortcomings, it's no consolation to hear that their ideas have been ignored, too! Many of them – especially if they have been there a while – have stopped even trying to make changes. Perhaps they don't believe they have the influence to make a real difference. Perhaps the Powerful Others (those in the boss's inner circle who act as his support base and source of reassurance – we'll come back to them) stymie your ideas or corrupt them to serve their own purposes. These Powerful Others will have a vested interest in maintaining the *status quo*. They may be fearful for their own positions or don't want anyone else to gain influence with the boss.

POWER BEGETS BELIEF

You've probably already tried to change your boss's mind – and you have almost certainly found it difficult, if not impossible. In 2006, Briñol and his colleagues wrote in the *Journal of Personality and Social Psychology* that power makes people more confident in themselves and much less likely to be swayed by argument. Brian is a good example of this: he has been in charge for many years and the company has undoubtedly done well under him. He's come to trust his own judgement above anyone else's – so why should he listen to someone as inexperienced as Jo? Especially when her approach doesn't resonate with his instincts.

NO TWO BOSSES ARE ALIKE

If you are dealing with an out-and-out despot (a rare beast, but they do exist), this can become a self-fulfilling circle. He has power, leading to a sense of invincibility and infallibility (hubris), possibly feeding a more dictatorial management style, which leads to even less devolvement of power. In such cases, these beliefs, often bearing only a tenuous relationship with reality, result in perceptions of omni-competence and infallibility.

Perhaps your own boss isn't quite so dictatorial. He might simply be afraid of change or confrontation with his subordinates, peers or line managers. Alternatively, he might take comfort from known routines and processes and be reluctant to make decisions that vary these.

Whatever the reason behind his reluctance to change, the result is the same for you and for other forward-thinking people in the company: frustration!

You may think you know what your organisation needs to do to succeed, but what seems obvious to you might not even be entertained by your boss. What can you do to steer your company in the direction it needs to go, if the boss simply wants you to execute the decisions he's already made?

Perhaps you have suggested some simple procedural changes, but even these have been bounced back. Not a good start – let's look at Jo's experience...

> "Brian, can we have more staff meetings?" Jo asked. "This'll help us check that we're all on the same page with our work and to nip any problems in the bud. We might also get some group input."
>
> Brian wasn't at all keen. "No! We've tried these before and they don't work. All that happens is that the staff end up having a group whine. It's a waste of time. Everyone should know what they're meant to be doing anyway."

Your insights are not less valid because you may have come from outside your current organisation. In fact, your fresh perspective may be just what the business needs. Your boss, however, will probably tell you that your organisation is unique. While there will always be some truth in this, it is also true that if you dig deep enough into the processes within any organisation, they will share common themes and needs with other organisations either generally or specifically within its sector.

Your organisation may have the potential to be great, but do you have the influence to make the changes needed? What critical success factors are missing? A lack of business planning can be addressed relatively easily but a lack of vision beyond the mere maintenance of the *status quo* will require less readily-available business or strategic skills. Will you be able to find these when you need them?

A GOLDEN THREAD?

In all areas of management, there are general themes e.g. personnel development, line management, delegation, communication. Some managers get so bogged down in the specifics of their own business that they lose sight of the common themes. Landing a man on the moon or coaching a football team, while very different activities, have common management needs. Both sets of team members require a sense of importance in their work, a greater or lesser degree of autonomy and a common purpose. Gravitational differences between the moon and the earth (or the offside rule!) are part of the mix, of course, but focusing on these won't give you the teamwork and effective communication needed for success.

Depending on the kind of boss you have, you will probably encounter one or more of the following problems:

- inadequate or absent planning;
- lack of benchmarking and/or clear goals;
- poor staff morale and retention, with attendant financial implications;
- disempowered managers, insufficient interaction with management and poor reporting structures;
- ill-chosen management, strategic and leadership philosophies;
- team-building deficits;
- personal issues and/or agendas between senior managers and the boss;
- an overriding and unsustainable profit imperative;
- fear of change;
- mismatch between espoused values and real values (hidden agendas).

THEMES, NOT INSTRUCTIONS

This book has been written to give you a thematic focus and a framework within which to operate. With few exceptions, we will not deal with the details of specific issues, nor will we attempt to give you a step-by-step account of how to deal with every hurdle. This is deliberate. We believe it is better to develop a thorough understanding of concepts and principles before applying them to specific situations. If you have a good conceptual grasp of these themes and their interrelatedness, then you will be able to develop your own methods by which to apply them. Because you have developed these yourself in your own context, you will be able to greatly increase your effective scope and flexibility when dealing with day-to-day issues within your own organisation.

We could try to outline every imaginable scenario you might encounter but, we're sure you'll agree, that would make this book both enormous and terribly tedious! What will work much better is to equip you with the concepts you need. Imagine, if you will, learning how to ask directions in a foreign language. You might learn how to ask the question in that language, and what a sample answer might be. But if you're actually visiting that country and using the language, and the answer is given in a different way to the way you've learnt, you won't be able to understand it! Knowing the language better and understanding the various ways the answer might be given would give you a much better chance of success. The same applies to what we're describing.

We've divided the book into thematic sections to help you to order your thoughts and to formulate a plan for the situation in which you find yourself. In order to help make some of the book's concepts more relevant and understandable, we have also included a number of case studies and anecdotes.

OUR MASTER PLAN

This first chapter is an overview of the problems you're encountering and introduction of the concepts we'll be discussing.

Chapter 2 looks at the boss, the various ways in which he (or she) can behave, some of his strengths and weaknesses and how you can work most effectively with him.

Chapter 3 deals with the history of the organisation and how it's come to be the way it is now. We look at how ideas become entrenched and how an organisational culture develops.

Chapter 4 concentrates on the importance of having a plan: knowing what you want to achieve and how you intend to achieve it. Once goals have been set, how do you measure progress towards these – and how do you know if you've achieved them?

Chapter 5 engages with the reasons for resistance to change. How does this happen and why, and what you can do to overcome it.

Chapter 6 is all about the organisation as it is now: what capabilities it has, what human, intellectual and physical resources it can draw on and whether or not this gives it the potential to be great. Is taking on this task worth your while? In particular, we look at what many great companies have in common and how you can help your organisation to acquire those attributes.

Chapter 7 concerns itself with your own assets. Changing the direction of an organisation requires great effort and skill, and it's important to evaluate whether or not you have the ability to take this on. Emotionally, intellectually and, quite probably, physically, this will be a big challenge requiring outside support – do you have what it takes?

Chapters 8 and 9 are all about sales. We believe selling

in the broadest sense, including selling an idea, is critical for success. We look at some basic principles and techniques in Chapter 8 and then expand on them in Chapter 9.

Chapter 10 brings all these concepts and ideas together. It looks at how, in practical terms, to implement the changes you need and the issues you might encounter in doing so.

Chapter 11 contextualises all the information outlined above into a model for managing change.

Chapters 12 helps you to understand why, at first, you need a huge effort to get things moving while later it takes so much less effort to maintain the momentum.

The final chapter, 13, concerns itself with the most important person of all: you! We'll help you make the changes you and your organisation need but, more than that, this book will help you to grow and develop as a manager and as a person.

STAY OR GO?

Just like you, Jo has a fundamental question to answer: should she stay or should she go? Would she be better off packing her Moleskine and her Blackberry, waving goodbye to Brian and heading off somewhere more promising? Happily for Jo, she meets up that night with her great friend Charlotte, who advises her on how to make this very important decision. Charlotte is older than Jo and is an accomplished manager of many years' experience. They have a regular Friday night date at their local wine bar for a *post mortem* of the week's trials and tribulations. Jo has just finished pouring her heart out to Charlotte about her frustrations with Brian's intransigence:

> "But I remember how excited you were when you started!" objects Charlotte. "You were chuffed to bits to get Brian as your boss. You've been talking about Simian forever!"
>
> "I know, Charlie, but I'm so disappointed. To be honest, I'm amazed how well they've done with Brian at the helm."
>
> Charlotte is intrigued. "Is Brian really as bad as you think? He can't be! Maybe you're missing something about him. Or about Simian?"
>
> Jo ponders this. "There are some really good people there," she says, "and they seem frustrated, too. But I guess you're right. There must be something about Brian I've missed."

Whether your boss is really as bad as he seems is a very important question. And Charlotte is absolutely right to ask it. We'll look at types of bosses in more detail in Chapter 2.

THAT'S JUST THE WAY IT IS...

Charlotte goes on to raise another important question:

> "Have I told you the story of the ten monkeys?" asks

Charlotte. "It's all about how we can fall into strange habits without realising."

Jo has always liked Charlotte's ability to tell entertaining tales with a moral. So she pours herself another glass of Pinot Grigio and settles back to hear the story...

"So the ten monkeys were put in a cage with a banana hanging from the ceiling and a stepladder under the banana. The ladder was strategically positioned in such a way that the monkeys could reach the banana by going up the stepladder. It didn't take very long before one of the monkeys twigged to this and headed for the stepladder. As soon as he touched the stepladder, he and the other monkeys in the cage were sprayed with a high-pressure water hose – like a fire hose. The monkeys quickly realised that any touch of the stepladder would result in this negative stimulus. So eventually they all settled back in the cage, looking longingly at the banana but with nobody going close to the stepladder.

"The researchers then took one monkey out of the cage and replaced him with another who had not been exposed to the high pressure water treatment. After a few minutes he quickly summed up the situation and saw all the other monkeys obviously missing a trick by not using the stepladder to get to the banana. Thinking himself to be a bright button, he headed for the stepladder. Before he could get his foot on the first rung of the stepladder, all the other monkeys beat him vigorously because they were scared they were going to get sprayed again.

"Within a short period he realised that touching the stepladder would result in a beating and he gave up trying to get to the banana. Gradually, one by one, all the sprayed monkeys were replaced by monkeys who had not been sprayed until eventually they had a cage full of monkeys who had never been sprayed for approaching the stepladder. But, should any monkey make even the slightest attempt to touch the stepladder, he would be beaten. Why? None of them knew, but that's the way things were done around here!"

Another good point, Charlotte! We'll be looking in more detail at how organisations develop their idiosyncrasies in Chapter 3.

"That's all well and good, Charlie, but my problem is now! I'm not that bothered about the whys and wherefores. I've got to deal with him again on Monday! I'm tearing my hair out! Why won't he change?"

Good work, Jo. Resistance to change will be covered in Chapter 5. Over the course of the evening (and another bottle of wine), Charlotte and Jo will tease out the rough framework that we'll be following in this book. This includes assessing the potential of the organisation and how to develop it, a critical self-evaluation (both of your abilities and your ideas for the organisation), techniques for influencing and persuading people within and outside the organisation and how to implement the changes that are needed.

But let's start where they did, with the boss.

THE BOSS, AND STARTING TO DEAL WITH HIM

THE CRUNCHY BIT:

It's easy to dismiss your boss as some kind of dinosaur. Don't. He became the boss for a reason: his own skill set. Annoying as he may now seem, he had skills and abilities that the company needed at a particular time – and probably still needs. And he knows an awful lot about what has and hasn't worked in the past. This knowledge could be critical if you want to avoid falling flat on your face at the first hurdle!

In order for you to deal with your frustration you need to understand your boss – or at least understand him a little better. This will help you to understand your company. It is, after all, made in his image. And, if you know his strengths and weaknesses, worries and ambitions, you are much better placed to present your ideas in a way that's likely to be acceptable to him.

In this chapter we give you some simple insights into your boss' personality type. Is he a Results Rupert (bad side: win at all costs / good side: get the job done), Detail Danny (analyse everything to death / no nasty surprises), Likable Larry (avoids confrontation with anyone / keeps a stressed team together) or Excitable Eric (liable to fly off the handle every five minutes / gets everyone enthused)? You can, of course, use the same analysis on your allies. But use them on your family and friends with care if you want to keep them!

Understanding the boss is all very well, we hear you say, but you don't have a year to do an in depth analysis. You want to start making changes now.

Fair enough. You'll be delighted to hear that this chapter ends with a short checklist of things you can do today to 'persuade through involvement' i.e. increase his levels of engagement, reduce his resistance to change and give your ideas the best chance of success. This is not a substitute for understanding him, but may speed up the process of change a little.

ANNOYING? YOU BET!

It's often said that people join an organisation but leave a boss or manager.

As we explained earlier, the behavioural traits and characteristics that got your boss to where he is now are not necessarily those that are required at this level of leadership. Previous success can get in the way of future success. The core issue is identifying the key workplace habits that he needs to break. In his 2008 book *What Got You Here Won't Get You There*, Marshall Goldsmith identifies a number of habits we all would be wise to avoid:

- The need to win at all costs – even when it doesn't matter

- Adding "too much value" i.e. giving your opinion to every subject or idea that is discussed
- Clinging on to the past
- Not listening
- Refusing to express regret
- Failing to give proper recognition
- Claiming undeserved credit
- Failing to express gratitude
- Making destructive comments
- Negativity
- Starting sentences with '*no*', '*but*' or '*however*'.

Any of the above could be signs of poor leadership. But even poor leaders usually want their teams to show high levels of commitment. Unfortunately, they don't seem to be aware of what is required in order to get people on board. They can be stuck predominantly in the transactional side of leadership and may not understand that, while a punitive culture may result in some level of compliance, that compliance usually lacks commitment from most team members, especially the important ones. People find the continued absence of adequate reward and recognition exceptionally demotivating. Omnipotent conservatism in terms of reluctance to change (see *The Parable of the Ten Monkeys* in Chapter 1) isn't very motivating or inspiring, especially if you're a self-starter.

Brian may now be an obstacle to progress and could even be holding the organisation back. His core skill set remains intact, but he refuses to relinquish control even of areas that are not within his main sphere of expertise.

In Jo's example, Brian might insist on overseeing a creative project when his expertise lies in customer relations.

WHAT GOT YOU HERE WON'T GET YOU THERE…

All this may be true but you should not lose sight of the fact that the boss may still possess valuable insight into the nuances of running this business. There may have been good reason for the protocols, policies or approaches that you think are simply wrong or outdated. Perhaps they're still valid, but for reasons you don't understand.

It is likely that your boss is not a nasty man. He may be very bright, capable and ambitious. He will, very probably, have a commanding presence, possess many good leadership abilities and likely have a detailed understanding of the organisation and its history. In many respects he is a good guy who is not holding you back out of sheer bloody-mindedness. He might genuinely see risks in what you're proposing and really not see anything wrong with the organisation or team that he is leading right now.

People are complicated. You and I might be easy to get along with and consistent in our approach and reactions (aren't we?), but we know that everyone else tends to be more challenging. Your boss is no exception.

In order to manage people effectively, we need to understand them. This sounds like basic management advice, but we're going to apply it upwards, to your boss.

NOT ALL BAD

Do you really understand your boss's personality, his skills and abilities? If you can, you will find working with him a lot easier. Looking at different personality types, and how to support, reinforce or empower each one, will give you a good start in dealing with him.

The 'Brian' in our book is a caricature. We've deliberately exaggerated his negative qualities for dramatic effect. We've done so to show the various ways in which almost any boss can obstruct or interfere with new ideas. It may be because he is afraid of change or because he's indecisive. He may feel threatened by you. Or he may simply be a power-hungry megalomaniac. There could be all sorts of different reasons. But the end result is always the same – you are effectively blocked in your ambitions for the company.

There are any number of theories and models of personality types. All of them are simplifications and no-one's personality is entirely represented by any one type. No, not even your boss! The models add value by giving you a way to *start* looking at people and thinking about how best to approach them. The simple, four-part example we use gives enough detail to be helpful, and is based on a few very well established models (Wilson Learning's *Social Styles* model, Thomas International's *Personal Profile Analysis* and Cameron's *Competing Values Framework*).

Using our model, Brian can be seen to be weak in some areas and have strengths in others. He may be competitive, competent and focused – and be very effective because of this. But he could end up not completing projects, neglect quality, be poor at problem solving and resistant to change.

Another boss might be friendly, enthusiastic and sociable, embracing change and creativity, but be poor at conflict management or shy away from performance management or involvement in challenging interpersonal situations.

You might think that your own boss is caring, encouraging and great at relationships but conservative, averse to conflict and poor at decision-making or giving negative feedback. Yet another boss might exude confidence and knowledge, and excel when it comes to performance, reliability and efficiency. This one's shortcomings stereotypically include an inherent conservatism, coldness, aloofness and an infuriating attention to detail prior to any decision-making.

Your boss may even be an exasperating mix of one or more of the above. At times, he may lean towards one stereotype then frustrate you by switching to another. People can be complicated! Whatever he is, you still have to deal with him.

FOUR BOSSES WALK INTO A BAR…

Let's unpack these styles in a little more detail. We focus first on the negative traits to mirror your frustration, but bear in mind that each style has its benefits, too. Please remember that these styles are caricatures. Any of us might fit best into one type or another, but it's unlikely that you, or your boss, would match every single part of the descriptions that follow. We've chosen exemplars who, for us, demonstrate some key elements of each type, but don't expect them to match every part of the description any more than you, we or your boss would.

The **Results Rupert**-type is outcome-focused and incredibly demanding and pushy. He has a tendency to be overbearing and to disregard the opinions of others, with an overblown belief in his own abilities. He'll stop at nothing to get what he wants, and this type isn't always above using dirty tactics to get it.

Your perception may be all about the negatives, but don't forget that Rupert is happy to put in huge hours, focusing all his energies on getting a result. His competitive streak can be great in gaining a corporate advantage. When the chips are down, having a Rupert on your side can be a great advantage.

Steve Jobs, a typical 'Rupert', created a very commercially successful company. His clarity of vision and determination brought great financial rewards. If he was a Rupert, though, no-one in his company would have liked him and they'd not have been willing to make any extra effort for him.

As 'Window to Wall Street' (http://windowtowall street.com/applehistory.aspx) neatly puts it, Steve Jobs was "A Visionary – A Freedom Fighter – A Pirate – A Tyrant". None of this takes away from his success, but was there a human cost?

A **Likable Larry**, on the other hand, cares about

making sure everyone gets along. The downside can be struggling to make up his mind and potentially going to any lengths not to rock the boat. He can be stubborn, slow to make decisions and even slower to change direction once the course is set.

His strengths are his genuine desire to look after his team and to make sure that everyone feels heard and understood. His management style is participatory, his team loves him and his followers are prepared, almost literally, to lay down their lives for him.

Nelson Mandela, an example of this leadership style, demonstrated many of these traits in taking South Africa from a worldwide pariah and despicable experiment in social engineering to a beacon of democracy and unity for the world. But, by failing to impose discipline in the ANC, most famously with his wife, Winnie Mandela, did he inadvertently sow the seed for future discord within that organisation?

The ANC has undergone many bouts of pretty public infighting over the years, including recently when one of their very popular youth leaders publicly mocked the President of South Africa and head of the ANC (http://vancouversun.com/business/mandela+party+falter s+infighting+splits+South+AAfrica/5953634/story.html).

Detail Danny has too many questions for his own good. He's the ultimate nitpicker – analytical to the extreme. He's easily seen as insensitive, distant and can overlook the feelings of others. He often appears cold, aloof and reserved.

His approach, though, ensures that nothing is

overlooked – think of Barack Obama. Planning will be thorough and methodical, minimising the risk of a crisis. His formal style lends an air of competence to his activities.

Detail Danny can be great when the details are important. His focus may ensure that nothing is forgotten, but the bigger and more complex the problem the more detail he may need. A crisis can bring total paralysis.

A good example of this was Mr Obama's lengthy strategy review on Afghanistan. This, according to *Time* magazine's Swampland column, led to great frustration among European leaders as well as back home in the USA. (http://swampland.time.com/2009/10/19/the-afghan-strategy-review/)

Excitable Eric leaps from one idea to the next without any focus or planning. He's easily distracted and often indiscreet.

Eric has his positives – a bit like Oprah Winfrey. His charisma stems from his great enthusiasm, unending supply of ideas, infectious energy and outgoing nature.

Eric's energy and enthusiasm can be draining! A stream of good ideas is all very well, but he often lacks the stamina to see anything through to completion.

People may love Excitable Eric's positivity, but his lack of ongoing focus can be frustrating. For example, he may not be interested in the practicalities required to make his dreams a reality, ignoring the mundane present in favour of his dreams of the idealised past or of the future.

The Jobs, Mandela, Obama and Oprah type each has its place in making a success of any organisation. Given the right circumstances, each style has the potential to become a boss. But, without the flexibility to adapt to changing circumstances, each can easily become a liability and stifle the very growth it helped to create.

YOUR BOSS HAS THE POWER!

But back to your boss... Added to his personality type is the power that's come with his position. This positional power in itself makes change more difficult. For example, as we said in Chapter 1, psychologists have found that power makes people more confident of themselves and much less likely to be swayed by argument. It's a self-fulfilling circle: the boss has power, leading to a sense of invincibility and infallibility, feeding a more dictatorial management style, which leads to yet more power. Scientific research has conclusively demonstrated that people in positions of power have confidence in what they are thinking and this makes them unlikely to change their position. Power makes people more likely to believe unquestioningly in their own ideas. If people are more conscious of their power before receiving an argument, they are more confident of their existing position and become even more difficult to persuade.

A boss that takes all power to himself effectively disempowers his staff. It doesn't matter whether he's done this on purpose or if it's an unconscious effect. Part of your task in helping your organisation to succeed despite your boss will be to re-empower your staff. And, strange as it may seem, your boss may need support and empowerment in areas where he is weak. We'll look at examples of how each of our personality types might benefit from empowerment.

Jo remembers a 'conversation' she had with Brian that demonstrates disempowerment in action:

"Jo!"

Brian's called Jo in for a discussion prior to her meeting with a potential new client, Andrew. Brian's met Andrew before but failed to get the account. He's worried that they might miss out again but he can't take the meeting himself because of a diary clash.

"Andrew's a tricky customer," says Brian. "He'll be wanting a good deal. Last time he couldn't make up his mind in spite of everything I told him. I spoke to him for over two hours. He still didn't understand what I could do for him! You have to make him understand that we're the only company that can do this work properly. We've got everything he needs and I've been doing this for years and years! He just needs to trust us – and not interfere.

"When he starts going on about social media platforms, you just tell him that that's the wrong place for his brand. If he disagrees with that, show him what we did for CorporateKidz last year. That social media stuff just won't work for him.

"One more thing: I won't be around for this – I've got to collect my daughter for her music lesson. If

Andrew wants anything I haven't covered, run it by me before you agree anything."

In fact, this 'conversation' with Brian went on for over three hours. Jo emerged feeling completely overwhelmed and deflated. She'd been looking forward to getting to know Andrew, understanding his needs and developing a campaign for him. The last thing she expected was chapter and verse from Brian on how to deal with every detail of the meeting.

Jo's also as sure as she can be that the meeting won't go according to Brian's script and that she won't be able to contact Brian when she needs to. She feels anxious, disempowered and insecure when she should be looking forward to meeting a potential new client. Disempowerment in action, indeed!

BusinessDictionary.com defines empowerment as the *"management practice of sharing information, rewards and power with employees so that they can take the initiative and make decisions to solve problems and improve service and performance. It is based on the concept of giving employees skills, resources, authority, opportunity and motivation, as well holding them responsible and accountable for outcomes of their actions."*

As we've said, it may not only be the staff who need empowerment, but also your boss. In an interpersonal sense, empowering Brian to listen more to others will allow him to focus on the client and improve his understanding of the client's needs. We'll look at this and other aspects of empowering and influencing people in due course.

Over time, you may need to help him gain skills to be a better boss and team member. Make sure that your efforts with the staff do not overlook the two most important players in this game – your boss and you!

CREATED IN HIS OWN IMAGE

Power in an organisation doesn't come only from a job title or position. It also comes, for example, from your ability to influence others to get the changes you want. The discussion on organisational cultures in Chapter 4 shows how power can manifest itself in surprisingly different ways. Your empowerment strategy should not be focused on deposing your boss. That's not the idea at all, and is unlikely to be achieved. Indeed, you might not even want that top position, just for the organisation to reach its potential.

As we said above, your boss reached the position he now holds because he does possess a certain skill set and did very well with the challenges he was faced with at the time he was rising through the organisation. His core skill set remains, but what is required are additional, sometimes complementary skills to move things to a higher level. This is an important conceptual point. Through altering and assisting the boss's development while encouraging an alternative organisational culture, you can help give others power and control without a direct frontal attack on the boss. By attempting an assault on his symbols of status and power, you take enormous risks, which might well cause your entire project to fail – and have you looking for another job!

With few exceptions, most people agree that the role of a boss has changed and will continue to change. Bosses have largely gone from being autocrats and dictators, like Mr Burns from *The Simpsons*, to being 'servant leaders', like Ghandi. Not all bosses have changed. Results Rupert, for example, for all his vision and charisma can be a pretty scary boss. The view that employees are children requiring a benevolent parent has largely been replaced by one of an entrepreneurial partnership. This requires empowerment initiatives, especially from the boss, if one wishes to optimise the team's productive ability.

Bosses have personality types. This is likely to be reflected in the management culture of the organisations they lead. Remember, though, that the personality types are great simplifications of reality and ignore individual subtleties and nuance. When any boss runs an organisation, that organisation's management structure and culture will over time come to reflect his personality and style.

TAKE A LONG LOOK IN THE MIRROR

The Centre for Management and Organization Effectiveness (CMOE) has come up with a classification of employer-employee relationships that we find particularly insightful.

- **Adversarial**

A model based principally and traditionally on the military, where people are viewed as just another resource along with equipment and buildings. In this model, people are taught not to think but simply to submit to authority. This often breeds resentment, boredom and dependence on the boss.

Depending on the boss's personality type, this dependence may actually serve as some form of affirmation. How empowering to have your minions unthinkingly carry out your every directive! The question that must be asked, however, is, *"What price does the organisation pay for this?"* Unfortunately, the historical and niche success of this model has led to its continued application.

A military unit is a good example of this, but you might also find it in a small family business that's grown larger. Henry Ford's original approach to car manufacture tended to fall into this category: just as car parts were interchangeable, so were people.

This can be a very effective means of running a small company. As an organisation grows in size, however, it also gains complexity and a command-and-control approach will limit its ability to engage with staff, reduce client care and impact adversely on the bottom line.

- **Patriarchal**

This is a benevolent dictatorship. Despite having control, the boss means well and really believes he knows what's best for the employee – and, for employee, you could read 'child'. In closely-knit smaller organisations, this may be seductive and leads employees to believe that if they keep their heads down and don't ask a lot of questions, they will get ahead and things will work out. The downside of this is that innovation and risk-taking is not encouraged, which may be seen as a good thing by *late adopters* (see Chapter 3). Power and control lie in the 'parent's' hands.

David Brent, the boss in the hit television series *The Office*, is an example of this style. He really does want to look after his staff and help them, but does so in a condescending and patronising manner.

Staff, in this model, have little room to stretch or grow their abilities and talents. While the model will undoubtedly suit some workers, it is easy to understand why the application of this framework results in independent thinkers feeling robbed of their aspirations, dreams and self-confidence.

While there may be more scope for the boss to listen, the same risks attend this model as the adversarial one.

- **Silent**

The prevailing attitude in this model is one of

apathy and neglect on the part of the boss. This can result in the staff being caught in one of the two models above, or using their own initiative. This commonly occurs when the boss reaches his position by virtue of a once-useful skill while failing to develop new skills. An example might be a software engineer finding himself in charge of a sales force because he wrote the software that the team uses.

Whatever the cause, employees feel unchallenged, neglected and unappreciated. The boss' experience and knowledge may even be revered – he could be a real leader in his field. But his knowledge and skill is not available to help employees grow and learn. A self-starter or one of the people with the right stuff (see Chapter 10) won't mind this set-up too much, as it can give them a lot of autonomy. The boss in this model isn't trying to keep all control in his own hands. Without the driver or self-starter, however, the team will have no direction. If the team is lucky enough to have a driver on board, he will likely end up running that section – with the boss's tacit approval.

Silence may sound like a bad thing – and it can be. But it can be effective in some organisations. For example, a UK doctors' partnership might run this way, with each doctor doing essentially the same thing.

- **Entrepreneurial**

This model is born out of a need for competitiveness. Here the boss maintains high accountability and autonomy whilst simultaneously collaborating with employees and providing purpose and meaning to their interactions. He is engaged and engaging. Problems are confronted in a supportive manner with successes being acknowledged and reinforced. Collaboration is focused on ensuring that any team member's performance is supported and optimized. This approach views employees as equals with a lot at stake in the workplace.

There are many examples of this style. For example, Microsoft in its early days was highly entrepreneurial, and Google remains so.

More than three decades' research by the CMOE has shown that a skilful boss relies less on authority and more on collaboration and negotiation. An effective boss uses his ability to reason, to ask penetrating questions and to listen. His title is not used as a weapon or even a tool. He will often confer with employees and understand instinctively (or perhaps through learning) that a dictatorial approach results in anger, resentment and a withdrawal of support and co-operation. Whilst some degree of compliance may be evident, this will remain only as long as there is supervision. The entrepreneurial approach focuses on helping everyone to reach their potential within the context of teamwork. A partnership, in theory, should help this entrepreneurial model to flourish. While partnerships don't always guarantee an easy ride, they do increase the likelihood of being able to overcome problems and deal with difficulties in good time. Of our four alternatives, this style leads to the highest level of staff engagement.

While the adversarial and patriarchal leadership models may work for a particular boss on a personal, ego level, many bosses would like to benefit from high levels of employee engagement, commitment and motivation. Unfortunately, he may not understand that any of the following can also contribute to the development of adversarial, patriarchal or silent models:

- an overly punitive culture
- a lack of adequate reward and recognition
- omnipotent conservatism
- an inability to communicate a plan clearly
- an inability to delegate adequately
- a need for power and control
- a lack of freedom of speech

And that this will almost certainly result in a significant loss of people – especially the ones the organisation really needs.

We recommend that you carefully re-examine the processes and approaches you have been using when attempting to persuade the boss. We'll look at practical steps in dealing with the different personality types in coming chapters. Irrespective of types, however, there are some basic rules to remember when dealing with anyone in a position of power.

CORPORATE KUNG FU, LESSON 1

In presenting arguments to him try, as far as possible, to neutralise his power psychologically. Whenever possible, avoid meetings in his office (his seat of power), and make sure your introductory statements don't remind him of his authority or prompt him into thinking of past successes (e.g. I know you didn't like this idea last time, do you have any objection to…). Remember the point we made earlier – the more conscious he is of his power *before* being presented with an argument, the less likely he is to be persuaded.

When you have to challenge the *status quo*, you would be better off asking questions than making what the boss may perceive as critical, challenging or confrontational statements. We'll deal with this in our chapter on sales, later in the book. Prepare your questions carefully and take your time. You may choose to follow up with further well thought-out questions on a subsequent occasion rather than lose a debate that you needn't have engaged in at the first meeting. With a bit of luck (and a lot of design) you might get him to see the light all by himself – or an alternative even better than yours may emerge! It may not be kudos you're after. Allowing the boss time to integrate your question into his own thought process and then come up with your preferred solution all by himself is just fine – you're after change, not power.

Have another look at the end of Chapter 1. Notice how skilfully Charlotte steered Jo towards finding the answers by herself. Charlotte didn't try to TELL Jo, she helped her draw her own conclusions.

A couple of weeks on, Jo meets Charlotte again at their usual haunt. Jo seems somehow more relaxed this time, and Charlie is intrigued.

"So, Jo," asks Charlotte, "what's happening at work? You seem a little happier than before."

"You were spot on about Brian, you know," Jo acknowledges. "He's not the total disaster I thought. Now I've tried to get to know him a bit better, he's a bit more predictable."

Charlotte's pleased, "Cool! Tell me!"

"Well, he's still damn frustrating! But I'm getting the knack of how to put things in a way that's less threatening to him. Sometimes I present my idea as if he's thought of it! It's just so slow – like wading through treacle!"

"That's a start, at least," encourages Charlotte. "Why so slow? What's the holdup?"

Jo thinks a moment. "That's just Simian, I guess. There's people who influence Brian negatively. But there's a positive group, too. I need to think about it…"

You're on to a good point here, Jo. Simian is much more

than just Brian. Within any organisational culture there are subgroups of people, both positive and negative. We've looked at leadership styles and touched on how this can influence organisational culture. Now we need to understand how Simian got here. You, of course, need to understand how your own organisation developed the culture it has. Let's look at that in Chapter 3.

THE ORGANISATION 3

THE CRUNCHY BIT

You joined your company because of what it had achieved or what you believed it could yet accomplish. Now that you've started work, you've discovered that the organisation has its flaws – just like your boss has his! What it did well before may not be what it needs to do to achieve future successes.

We tell a great story in this chapter about learning to waterski – please read it! There we make the point that, to get better at something, you sometimes have to 'unlearn' old habits that previously served you well. Only then can you learn new ones.

Organisations are only as good as their people. The more people believe in what they're doing and the more engaged they feel, the better they perform. We show you how to identify those who can help you, how to help them to see the same potential in the organisation that you see, and how to engage them – to the benefit of all.

THE FUTURE'S BRIGHT. OR IS IT?

Let's look at what first attracted you to join the organisation that you now want to change for the better.

No-one joins a company they think is really, really rubbish! The organisation almost certainly seemed great before you joined, and probably for a while after you'd started. Only then did you start to see the problems endemic to it. By now, you're so busy fighting the alligators in the corporate swamp that it's possible you've little time for a much better endeavour: draining the swamp to drive them all away!

Don't misunderstand: we're not suggesting that your primary aim should be to kill or drive out any alligators, but you're reading this because you believe the organisation can be better and you want help in getting there.

One or more of the following scenarios were almost certainly significant in attracting you to your position:

*   From outside, the company, like SimianSynergy, was seen as a significant, visionary player in the market. Now that you've had a chance to look under the hood, you can see the problems.
*   You may have been head-hunted and courted for a specific skill set by precisely those who now, perversely, seem to be obstructing progress.
*   You may have held slightly unconventional beliefs or ideas about systems relating to your industry and seen strong similarities within the new organisation. This level of resonance led you to believe that because this organisation had arrived at similar conclusions to you, there was a likelihood that together you could realise a dream.

- You may have identified a number of issues that were obstructing progress, and thought you'd been given a fair degree of latitude with a remit of joining the team and helping make a difference.

Your company has been successful, at least as far as you could see from the outside. Now that you're part of it, it's becoming all too apparent that it has very little in the way of systems or processes in place to maintain that success. Alternatively, systems and processes might exist but be so reactionary or ill thought-out that the company is successful in spite of them. Below, we have highlighted some scenarios that might explain how this came about:

ONE STEP BACK, THEN TWO STEPS FORWARD

The 'founding fathers' of the organisation were rich in entrepreneurial talent and were able to create a critical mass. Now, however, they are continuing to apply the same systems and processes in an attempt to sustain the growth when it is obvious to you and to others, if not to them, that new processes are needed. In other words, **what got them here, won't get them there** – to the next level. For example, communicating with a small team is easily done by direct contact and word-of-mouth. As the organisation grows, the simple message given to your core team may be horribly skewed by the time it reaches all levels of the organisation. Consequently, new methods (memos, newsletters, emails, etc.) must be found to communicate effectively with a much larger and potentially geographically dispersed workforce. Alternatively, key players in the team may have had excellent **hands-on team management skills,** which are now less relevant when attempting to steer and influence a larger group and team in new circumstances.

Jo's had another run-in with Brian. She phones Charlotte in a fit of frustration and anger. "He's such a pig-headed bastard! 'No' is his first response to anything new."

"Damn!" says Charlotte. "He's probably terrified to change. Actually, I can imagine how he might feel.

"Have I told you about how I first learnt to waterski?" Charlotte asks. "I spent loads of time with my friends out on the water teaching ourselves how to waterski. There was no expert around and we learnt by trial and error. We started on two skis and gradually worked our way up to one ski.

"The next step was to try to do slalom, leaning from side to side behind the boat and moving through buoys. While I felt I was doing pretty well, I just couldn't complete the slalom course with the buoys, no matter how hard I tried. I just couldn't make it.

"So one afternoon, down by the river, I was chatting to someone who was an experienced competitive skier. He started talking to me about technique. Apparently, in order to ski well on one ski, you need to have your strongest leg forward. But, unfortunately for me, when I was teaching myself I somehow started skiing on one ski with my strong leg behind. So, while I was able to ski relatively well, I just couldn't raise my game while using the wrong technique. In order to develop, I had to unlearn that and relearn with my strong leg forward.

"The downside of this was that for a period of time my standard of skiing would be significantly lower than it presently was."

We know that many people need to unlearn things in order to move forward. If you want to be able to empathise and achieve a level of understanding of Brian's attitude, it can be helpful for you to identify when you were in a similar situation.

Let's move back to our discussion on how your organisation might have evolved. You may have been recruited by a dynamic group that includes an **innovator and a late adopter** working together as part of a team. The innovator asks "Why not?" and wants to try new ideas and pioneer paths not previously trodden. The inherently-conservative late adopter gives a million reasons why the project or idea is doomed to failure and prefers the security of the familiar. Together they make a formidable pairing. If, however, the innovator moves on and leaves power in the hands of someone who prefers to boldly follow where others lead, then this inherent conservatism may start to prevail in the organisation. Equally, you could have the opposite situation with the innovator left in charge – leaving a trail of chaos in his wake and with no one prepared to pick up the pieces!

POWER TO THE PEOPLE?

Perhaps your organisation's **growth and success was at the expense of others** rather than through the support of others. People were seen as a disposable and easily renewable resource. If you didn't fit in, there would be someone else to take your place, and a prevailing belief that eventually the organisation would stumble upon the right person. You, on the other hand, have a **competing value system**. As we'll discuss later, management gurus are almost unanimous in saying that people are the critical success factor to any organisation or team. It is immensely valuable if you have the skills, experience and ability to help change things so that the human resources become viewed as pivotal in ensuring the ongoing success of the group.

Your boss has his own style, strengths and weaknesses, as we discussed in Chapter 2. Very importantly from the perspective of the organisation, the company will, to a greater or lesser degree, have formed in his image. It's important to look for this fingerprint when you evaluate the organisation, as you are doing now.

The whole organisation may be resistant to change because the boss is. If his default position is to defend the *status quo* and to point to the uniqueness of the environment in which your firm operates, the whole business may reflect this. He may be insecure, he may believe that he has to stick to his tried and tested methods or he may be wary of a loss of control – or any one of many other reasons. Understanding him, using the methods we discussed in Chapter 2, helps you to understand your organisation.

You joined your organisation because you could see its competitive edge and you knew it could be a market leader. And what is the most important factor in any organisation? People! The most valuable asset, the critical success factor. There has yet to be an organisation to have claimed greatness without the creativity, innovation, commitment and enthusiasm of the people who work for it.

A LONG AND HAPPY ENGAGEMENT

Human Resource Management has, for many years, claimed the 'asset management' role in this regard, securing success and growth through its people. We all know people who will do that little bit extra, and it's not always possible to point to a clearly definable cause. The reason for this is people going the extra mile. These people are essential because they have a direct or indirect impact on the bottom line. For example, the nurse who, unasked, brings a set of toys from her own home for the young child of the family keeping vigil at their sick grandmother's bedside, or the car rental agent who phones to see that you've arrived safely at your destination.

Like financial capital, people need to be treated with care, respect and commitment if the organisation expects them to stay invested and yield maximum return. Unlike financial capital, human capital is harder to measure. It can be influenced but not controlled. Consciously or unconsciously, employees weigh their commitment to their organisation and decide how much effort to put in. Effort over and above what's expected, like that of the nurse above, is called discretionary effort. This extra effort can result in two to three times the output from the same worker! This can, of course, have a huge effect on the bottom line. How much discretionary effort is expended by people in your organisation?

In the modern age, the way people feel about their work, and the discretionary effort they're willing to expend, is of increasing concern to all progressive companies. With very few exceptions, companies have downsized their workforce significantly and have to make the most of those that remain. There may be a few sectors that are lucky enough not to suffer from talent shortages. Most would agree, however, that finding the right staff is becoming increasingly difficult even in these times of high unemployment. Having found them, it makes sense to try to keep hold of your people. Also, if headcount has been cut back to the bone, productivity, innovation and levels of service delivery must all improve, and this will positively affect profitability. This is known as *employee engagement*. In the early 1990s, Sears turned from loss to profit in less than a year by engaging with their staff and receiving higher discretionary effort in return.

But true engagement can be a difficult path to follow. So, is it worth it? If this results in an increased level of commitment right across the workforce, the answer must be, "Yes!" Motivation and engagement almost always result in:

- improved productivity
- better working relationships
- lower staff turnover
- less absenteeism
- and better quality of work.

And that's got to be a good thing.

The above themes are designed to help you to understand the history of the organisation, to give you a filter through which to look at it. By understanding your company fully, you will be much better placed to make any changes. Context is everything. In this chapter, we're looking at the evolution of the company in the context of its human capital. Specifically, in terms of how it is currently failing to get the most from this capital. Later in the book we'll investigate the power of context in much more detail.

A truly engaged employee's positive attitude and behaviour will be noticed by clients and affect colleagues. This loyalty, focus, enthusiasm and initiative can be seen a mile off. People who are happy in their work become advocates for the organisation. A highly engaged company has a better performing workforce, enjoys higher staff retention, and delivers sustainable success through productivity and innovation, as well as being recognised as a pleasant place to work.

Since not everyone wants the same thing, creating an environment that fosters this positive behaviour is not easy. A common underlying theme is the emotional bond between the team and the organisation i.e. they understand the organisation's mission and vision and understand their role in relation to this. You, as a relatively new arrival, may lack this emotional bond, making your job that little bit harder. Ideally, one would like this to go even deeper i.e. their *values* are closely aligned with those of the organisation. If this level of engagement is reached there is a sense of 'community' within the organisation. For this to happen, the key lies in the quality of the personal relationships within the organisation. Don't forget that employees also know people, who in turn know more people – an obvious but often overlooked form of word-of-mouth advocacy and a source of new sales or recruitment.

EVERY ROSE HAS ITS THORN

To help understand what you, your boss or any other manager can do to try to facilitate this process, we'll look at leadership in two useful dimensions: transactional and transformational leadership. This relates directly to employee engagement, which is a reflection of the boss in the company he leads.

Transactional leadership involves rewards and incentives in exchange for behaviour that meets specific objectives. This form of leadership can play a role in shaping employee behaviour but won't usually result in the strong emotional bonds we described when talking about engagement.

Transformational leadership, on the other hand,

shares with the employees the importance of the company's targets. By understanding the mission or vision, or just the end point being aimed for, employees can work towards that goal. This process is led by the boss's ethical, honest and transparent behaviour. He sets clear goals and is enthusiastic about these. The staff, in turn, are encouraged to feel ownership of these goals and are trained and given development opportunities in order to reach them. The more the boss and the employees work together on a common pursuit, the stronger the bond between them, and the greater the engagement.

A lack of planning (or inability to clearly communicate a plan) can result in frustration – especially for the 'right' people. These motivated self-starters want to get out there and get the job done but may end up either being held up or in a conflicted position because their understood aim or objective opposes that of the boss. If this happens on the odd occasion it is unlikely to be significant but, if it's repeated over and over again, it may result in demotivation. The inability to delegate adequately causes motivated self-starters eventually to feel disempowered. While a larger number of people may succumb or assume a submissive stance simply waiting for instructions and exercising minor forms of initiative, most self-starters will move elsewhere so that their enthusiasm is not only encouraged but appreciated and rewarded.

The boss's need for power and control, which often results in micromanagement, is disempowering, demotivating and frustrating for competent and motivated staff. Objections, resistance to or frustration with the *status quo* voiced by the "right" people should be valued and encouraged. These are signs of engagement and a desire to improve things rather than primarily evidence of discontent. Unique and unconventional in-house solutions to the more common problems encountered in similar organisations (especially if they are obviously inefficient) will impact negatively on their credibility and frustrate those who have had meaningful experiences elsewhere.

Look out for personal agendas between key players. These can cause significant uncertainty and emotional conflict for the team. It can also be very demotivating and disempowering, especially if staff are caught in conflicting sets of instructions from multiple bosses or managers.

Are there hidden agendas in your organisation? If so, do you know why? You'll need to understand these if you're to understand your company. It's all very well to say the company is all about client care and service excellence, but if the staff perceive a naked profit motive, that will cause disengagement and discontent.

Jo seems to have moved from frustration to elation since the last time Charlotte saw her. She comes bouncing into the bar and plops herself down in Charlotte's booth.

"I've got it! I understand Brian better, and I know how Simian's problems developed. They're super-conservative because Brian's so afraid to change and he doesn't listen to anyone else's opinion. People feel helpless – they're not engaged at all! I just need to sort these out and…"

"Hold on! Hold on a minute!" smiles Charlotte. "You think you've got a handle on Simian, and how Brian's influenced that. Great! "What about the team? Do you really think that, if you sort Brian out, they'll be all fired up and good to go?"

That's another key point from our coach, Charlotte. A plan is vital. Without focus, you might end up with a group of talented, motivated, hard-working individuals all rushing off in different directions. What's needed is a common goal. This is the topic we'll cover in Chapter 4.

PLANNING

THE CRUNCHY BIT

Whenever you set out to do something, it's a good idea to know exactly what you want to achieve. If you've not identified what you want to do, how will you know when you've done it? The earlier you can identify your end point, and the clearer your vision of what that point is, the more likely you are to achieve it. It's also much easier to determine your next step if you know where you're starting and what the end product will look like. Where you start is with the organisation as it is, including, vitally, its culture.

Culture is a slippery beast. It's often made in the image of the leader. But there is an unspoken culture, too. Everyone will be aware of it at some level of consciousness and it's usually different to the formal one. The formal culture will often be a reflection of the mission, vision and strategy of the organisation. Being able to judge the degree of alignment and difference between the two cultures will give you very helpful insights into what changes will need just a little nudge – and what will have to have a sledgehammer taken to it!

While assessing the organisation, don't forget to have a look at their business plan. If you have no business plan, it's enormously helpful to develop one, but we accept that this may be beyond what you can currently control. Don't despair. There's plenty you can achieve without one.

You'll not get anywhere with your programme for change without people to support you. From the business plan, the mission, vision and strategy, and from the spoken and unspoken culture of your organisation, you should have a pretty good idea of the value put in the people who work there. If this is a key part of what the organisation does: great! If not, you'll need to work to change this.

There are many, many ways that this can go wrong. Obstacles are everywhere, and not just to culture change, but to your entire vision of what the organisation can become.

DOES ANYONE HAVE A MAP?

Why, we hear you ask, are we talking about planning so early in the process? Surely there are more pressing 'nuts and bolts' issues to deal with first?

Yes, of course there are all sorts of details to be addressed in order to get your organisation moving in the right direction. In order to get there, though, you need a clear idea of what, precisely, you're aiming for. This means clarity of purpose for you, from which your detailed plans and actions will flow. This is what Steven Covey calls "beginning with the end in mind" (*Seven Habits of Highly Effective People*). Once you know your destination, it's much easier to choose a path or know when you're heading in the right direction. Without a plan, you can easily have a 'boss bottleneck' where all decisions have to go through one person. A clear plan that is agreed by top management allows far more devolution of authority and decision-making.

This means that the organisation also needs a plan. What is the strategy or aim of the organisation now? Is that what you'd like it to be? If a clear strategy doesn't yet exist, you can contribute to the development of a culture that allows one to evolve. And, if there is already a strategy in place, it's worth checking that this considers the people employed and how to meet their needs. If their needs are met, they will deliver more for the company. People, after all, contribute both to the culture and output of the organisation.

It follows, therefore, that in order to move the organisation forward you need to understand its existing culture. If you understand the way things work now, you can plan and implement the changes needed to get you and the organisation to your chosen end point.

Jerry, Jo's partner, has been watching her struggles since she joined SimianSynergy. He's been very worried that she's bitten off more than she can chew and has been gently hinting that she should leave. Now that she's so full of energy, he's even more worried that she might be setting herself up for a fall.

"Come on, Jerry, it's really not that bad!" she argues. "Brian is much clearer to me, I know where Simian's come from and I can see the need for a plan. All that's left is for Brian to create the plan and we'll be good to go."

"Jo," sighs Jerry, "how many times have you come across businesses which function despite the management system, not because of it? Without understanding the current culture, any plan might exist in a vacuum. If the culture and the plan aren't aligned, there's no chance of the plan working."

Culture is important in that it influences organisational structure, providing consistency and order as well as determining the conditions for internal effectiveness. Relationships and performance are also affected by it. But culture can limit strategy.

Culture can be defined as the sum of traditions, values, beliefs and attitudes that, together, make up the persuasive context for the way things are viewed and determine how things get done within the company. It's the way things are done here. This will include working practices, how customers are viewed and how staff are treated. For example, the organisation might constantly reinforce the need for outstanding customer service. If the reception desk is found to be understaffed and customer service is suffering as a result (phones ringing for too long, long queues for attention, etc.), the organisation might respond by making more human resources available at peak times. That would be in line with the espoused values of the company: the culture is aligned with a value of delivering customer service.

WHOSE CULTURE IS IT, ANYWAY?

Culture can be both explicit and implicit – sometimes the way the staff work and feel is substantially different to the culture espoused by the boss and the Powerful Others. Whatever the case, culture has an impact on how people are motivated, how success or failure are defined, the prevailing leadership and management style, how decisions are made and, very importantly, how change is viewed.

You must also be cognisant of the fact that encouraging and improving workplace performance is dependent on the ability of the workforce to collaborate in meaningful and productive ways, for example as teams. But you won't get anywhere with your plan if you do not take into account that everyone must *want* to work together – including your boss.

Essentially, you need to find a way of fully understanding how the staff feel, and why. If you don't have your finger on this pulse, we would recommend consulting with either a good market researcher or, strange as it may sound, a sociologist to work on ensuring that your findings are as objective as possible and accurately reflect the way people think and feel.

There are very many ways one can approach this, some are more qualitative (what they feel – valued, rewarded, empowered) and others are more quantitative (how strongly do they feel it?). We would recommend a balance of both. The detail on precisely how you do this is critical: asking the wrong question or asking it in the wrong way can invalidate the results or give you deeply misleading information. The detail on how to set up a questionnaire or similar research tool is beyond the scope of this book, but we highly recommend getting expert help to avoid these pitfalls.

There is one other significant point to bring to your attention in this regard: people often tend to rush straight into questionnaires or unstructured interviews so that they have data they can analyse. Without going into the details of various research methodologies, sample sizes, validity, etc., we can simply say we would highly recommend you start out with some form of **qualitative** research and then use this as the basis to refine the approach and detail of the subsequent **quantitative** work. This will give you a reasonably good idea of what you are starting with, and may provide some important clues to the direction in which you would like to get the organisation to move.

A qualitative question, for example, might be, "How valued do you feel in the work that you do?" with a freehand answer. Quantitatively, you could add a range of possible responses on a scale from 'very valued' to 'not at all valued'. The questions themselves, as we have said, are very important. Please do spend time on getting these right, and ask for help if needed.

Please don't be disheartened if this is beyond the scope of what you feel you can reasonably achieve. It's not easy to hire a consultant to examine an organisation, especially if the boss is unaware of or hostile to the idea. You can get a pretty good understanding of the culture simply by speaking to people and observing their interactions with their superiors. The bigger the company, the larger the pinch of salt you should apply to these observations, of course, but they can be very helpful. In the end, a consultant or organisation-wide questionnaire might be nice to have, but they need not be mission critical. You can go a long way without them.

In some circumstances, in order to change an organisation you will need to change the culture. In these cases, you have to understand what the implicit culture of the organisation is – or what most people would like it to be! In essence, you need popular support for the appropriate culture, values and ethos, something we'll look at in more detail later. If you have that, the chances of achieving success are far greater. Of course, 'appropriate' is highly context specific and will vary from company to company.

Since culture change is not easy, you must apply a fundamental principle of the sales process: focus on the clients. ('Clients' here are the people you're trying to influence rather than the customers of the company.) If the culture change you are trying to achieve is not acceptable to the staff, you are very unlikely to get interest in your vision, or buy-in and support for your initiatives.

William Schneider (*Why good management ideas fail – understanding your corporate culture*) describes a number of common organisational cultures. You may find that one or more sound familiar to you. This may help you and others to understand your starting point in order to plan your path to a better future.

It is also possible that you already have an appropriate culture in place but need to get support for changes in systems and processes in order to allow it to blossom. For example, everyone wants to help at that busy reception desk, but the rules and processes get in the way of great customer service.

CULTURE CLASSICS

In a **Control Culture**, power and intimidation are the order of the day. Success depends on the boss and Powerful Others acquiring and keeping control and is measured by dominance – bigger is better. The management style here is prescriptive and systematic, highly objective (measurable) and bound by policies and standard procedures. The style of leadership is directive, assertive and commanding, with power being tied to position, role or title. "Do as I say because I'm the boss!" The culture of the organisation is hierarchical and decisions are taken methodically, objectively and impersonally. Change, where it occurs, is mandated from on high and the work climate is formal and serious. A good place to be a boss, but not necessarily to work!

You might expect this organisation to be dominated by a Results Rupert, a driver, but this is not necessarily the case. Detail Danny, the analytical, might also operate here, as might Excitable Eric (an expressive). Don't fall into the trap of thinking that a particular boss or style can only exist in a particular culture.

A **Competence Culture**, on the other hand, rewards excellence and, unsurprisingly, greater competence. Staff are motivated by achievements and rewards and their success is measured by being the best. Managers tend to be task-driven, rational, objective and highly efficient and report to visionary leaders who prefer to convince, persuade and challenge their subordinates. Power achieved through the development of expertise and decisions are taken analytically, in a detached and efficient manner. The culture of the organisation takes the form of a matrix, with change welcomed, being driven by goals and achievements. The intense, competitive work climate is not for everyone, though.

The closest fit to our boss types is probably the analytical Detail Danny, but Results Rupert, our driver, or Likable Larry, our amiable boss, could also do well here. Results Rupert, for all his temper and drive, could flourish in a culture that demands technical competence and delivery.

In a **Collaborative Culture** individuals are involved and motivated through their affiliation with the group. Success is achieved through building teams and the formation of positive and strong relationships with synergy being a perfect way to measure success. Managers are informal, participative and people focused demonstrating a coaching and team-building style of leadership with trust being an important feature. In a collaborative culture the strength and depth of relationships are reliable indicators of degrees of influence. The organisational culture here centres around the group with decisions being made through democratic or consensus oriented processes.

Change is welcomed and even called upon by groups. The work climate here is harmonious and trusting but people are nevertheless busy.

If individuals are motivated primarily through growth and prosperity, a **Cultivation Culture** is probably most appropriate. Here success is measured by the degree with which you have realised your personal potential and the culture strives to provide you with opportunities for growth. Managers are people driven, relaxed but focus on empowerment and demonstrate a commitment to building commitment focused on a common vision. Here charisma plays an important role in the development of power. Decision-making is subjective but laced with a strong commitment and dynamism. Again change is embraced and taken as given. Here you are likely to experience a lively, committed and compassionate work climate.

In the remainder of this chapter, we'll look at how to get from where you are now, as identified above, to where you want to be. You will need to decide on your end point as this is highly specific to you and your particular company and situation. Irrespective of the start point and end point, however, you will need to plot a route to get there, which is what we'll be doing now.

If you are to be successful in moving the organisation in the right direction, the importance and value of a clear plan is self-evident. Bear in mind, however, that planning is simply another piece of the puzzle: getting the organisation to where it needs to be. Your ultimate job is to put the pieces of the jigsaw together and, at the same time, to help everyone see this big picture from the same perspective. This common perspective is a manifestation of the culture of the organisation. People with a common set of values and a common goal will see a problem or challenge in the same way, allowing a much more positive and effective response than if they were all coming at it from different points of view.

EVEN THE LONGEST JOURNEY STARTS WITH A SINGLE STEP (SORRY!)

Subtle shifts in focus can often make significant differences to outcomes later on. Renowned life coach Tony Robbins uses a very powerful analogy to show clearly how minute differences at the start of a process can significantly impact on outcomes. He describes, for example, how miniscule differences at the point of impact when you hit a golf ball (angle, swing, power, etc.) can all have a huge effect on where the ball ends up! (Check out the video clip on YouTube under *Tony Robbins – Tiny Changes Mean Huge Results.*)

There have been many, many volumes written on strategy and planning and there are bound to be differences of opinion on exactly how to fit the pieces together. We have tried to summarise the theory here and are confident that, even if you have a slightly different theoretical perspective, our framework will allow for the incorporation of the principles required to achieve your desired goal i.e. a new order of priorities in your organisation.

Reading this is the easy bit. What is more difficult to achieve is some form of congruence between the stated ethos and values of the company, and the culture which is experienced at the 'coal face'. You don't necessarily need to come up with a mission statement or a business plan for your organisation. The discussion that follows is to give you a little insight into what these mean and how you can use them to further your ends. You may also find yourself in a position to influence the formulation of a plan, and having a bit of theoretical background will be useful to you.

NOW, HERE'S THE SCIENCE

Ideally, the mission statement should be clear and easy to understand, a statement of intent on who you are, what your offer is and how you intend to deliver it. A strong mission statement can also affect an organisation's bottom line. For example, Amazon's mission statement is, "To be Earth's most customer-centric company, where customers can find and discover anything they might want to buy online, and to offer its customers the lowest possible prices." (Amazon, 2014). It should be something that the entire team can easily buy into. If every action of the entire team is centred around a common focus to which they are committed, the organisation will benefit from high levels of motivation and an improved customer experience. Interestingly, Dan Pink (http://www.youtube.com/watch?v=u6XAPnuFjJc) has shown that employees who believe in their company's mission feel happier in their jobs, irrespective of salary. This is especially true if they feel that their role is of value to the company. However, this benefit can only be realised if the mission statement is understood by all and the activities of the company and its managers do not contradict this. An example of such a contradiction might be a company that says how important its customers are but fails to respond to long queues at a checkout point in order to save on overtime.

This attachment to the mission will result in greater bonding to the organisation which will, in turn, impact positively on those indicators used to assess the success of the company, for example, productivity, profitability, turnover, word-of-mouth referrals, staff attrition and absenteeism.

A company's vision is what it would like the future to look like if it achieved its mission exceptionally well every day. In Amazon's case, that would be "to be Earth's most customer-centric company." Although Amazon put this ambition as the first part of their mission statement, they have, in fact, merged their vision and mission into a single statement. Your vision might be expressed in terms of customer perceptions, market share or other desirable outcomes. If people have bought into the mission, there is no reason why they shouldn't happily support the vision. The role of management should principally be to tweak perspectives subtly and to help remove anything that stands in the way of the team supporting this.

Strategy is a long-term plan of action designed to achieve a particular goal. Strategy follows on from vision and mission because it helps the team members more fully understand the practical steps necessary to get there. It also provides a template or guide to exactly how the vision is to be realised i.e. the tactics (behaviours, intentions) that will help you. The strategic plan should be the backdrop against which all organisational decisions are made.

If you wish to delve into more detail, a business plan is the next logical step. This should reflect the strategic intention of the organisation regarding the precise nature of responsibilities and resource allocation (e.g. budgets) necessary to achieve the desired effect within a specific time frame. Given that much can change within relatively short periods of time, most business plans usually tend only to cover a year in any great detail.

The value of a plan is that it demonstrates exactly how resources are intended to be deployed in the current macro- and micro-economic environment. Should a specific situation change, this change can readily be assessed in terms of impact on the plan and the deployment of resources adjusted to best achieve the original strategic plan in the altered circumstances. This may seem a little theoretical or academic to you, but it's included here simply to give background. Many excellent resources exist on business planning if you'd like to take it further. Banks, for example, as well as other lenders and the stock exchanges all put great value on business plans.

It is critical that the plan is seen in the context described above. The preparation of a business plan without the overarching context of mission, vision and strategy is likely to be dismissed very quickly as a waste of time whenever a change in circumstances requires any alteration.

PLAN TO SUCCEED

The benefits of using the planning process in this way are that:

- it encourages a regular and critical review of the entire business in a thorough and systematic way

- it helps you to spot potential pitfalls
- it can help you structure the business finances more efficiently
- it gives you the opportunity to plan and focus development efforts
- it functions as an objective measure of your success
- it devolves control away from the boss bottleneck (see above)

Whether your organisation finally goes for the traditional Annual Business Plan or leans towards Kaplan and Norton's Balanced Scorecard approach is less important than its actually committing to the process.

Before we move on to what oils the wheels of the entire process (ethos, values and culture) we would like to introduce one small but very significant perspective. This perspective is critical to the long-term success of any organisation and must never be overlooked in favour of mere numbers. What we are talking about is **preserving and enhancing the true assets of the organisation**.

Organisations, like people, need to produce results. To do this continually, they need to preserve and enhance the assets that first allowed them to achieve those results. A business' assets can be considered to be physical, financial and human, and the organisation's ability to deliver will be determined by the condition of these three resources. By and large the majority of the resources required to deliver results cost money i.e. they show up on the 'expense' side of a profit and loss account. When one focuses on the numbers, it may be easy to succumb to the illusion that by reducing expenses one can increase profits. Whilst this approach may improve short-term profitability, the possibility exists that service delivery could be adversely affected, resulting in a more negative customer experience, in turn causing a loss of turnover. In fact, fostering a strong organisational culture is an effective way for firms to increase their profit margins through cost reductions associated with improved employee satisfaction (e.g. lower absenteeism and reduced staff turnover). It follows that it is necessary to consider the value of the human capital of the business. It's preferable to concentrate any efficiency drives on first making cuts in waste and inefficiencies, not with cutting jobs. After all, motivated, capable, interested and creative workers are the best assets an organisation can have, especially when they are devoted to achieving organisational goals.

As we've mentioned previously, those who handle figures (e.g. accountants, economists) can find factors like job satisfaction highly subjective, so it may be difficult for them to understand their importance to business success. However, the presence and quality of factors such as job satisfaction and contentment are highly predictive of the likelihood of an employee remaining with the organisation, alongside higher levels of productivity and reduced rates of absenteeism. And all of these drive the bottom line!

Most people who lead or manage organisations got there through the operational ranks, promoted because of their application of operational skills. They were probably reasonably effective managers who made good operational decisions, but didn't spend much time thinking about the direction of the company. Consequently, many have not yet practised or acquired the skills of being an organisational strategist.

As we said earlier, these managers have skill sets that have stood them in good stead and have allowed them to rise in the organisation. These skills were very useful at that time, but may not be the ones needed to get to the next level. In fact, they may actually become impediments to progress: trying to keep using a hammer when you need a screwdriver will actually make things worse. They become obstacles to strategic thinking!

KEY OBSTACLES TO THINKING STRATEGICALLY

- **The strategists suffer from a blurred perspective**
  People in upper management positions often spend a lot of time together and rarely have any meaningful interaction with people at the coal face. This perspective is alienated from the reality experienced by staff and, critically, customers. For example, Brian's perspective is likely to be different to Jo's, as Jo is closer to the staff and the action.

- **Operational thinking predominates**
  Operational decisions and not strategic ones take

up the bulk of the time. Too much time is given to nuts and bolts issues, and not enough to planning strategy. There are always 'fires' that need extinguishing and these urgent issues command a lot of attention. Success at fire fighting becomes a self-perpetuating culture, and seen as a measure of organisational efficiency. Is there a fear that the company's fire fighting skills might be undermined by changes to the *status quo*? That queue at the checkout, for example, demands an immediate response. A reactionary response might be to worry that spending extra time thinking will result in not being available to act. In this case, trying to predict surges in demand for checkout counters could result in us not having the time to open another till!

Operational thinking or decision-making also tends to be focused on the short-term. And, because taking strategic decisions now will almost certainly result in operational matters having to be reviewed later on, there is a reluctance to make the strategic decisions that are needed. Furthermore, since some operational decisions can also have long-term effects, many succumb to the illusion that the operational decisions they made were, in fact, strategic.

• A reactive tendency
The doors are open for 'business as usual' and changes are principally made in response to external factors. These might be changes in

competitor pricing, legislation, orders placed or even macroeconomic changes e.g. a recession. Ultimately, the underlying thinking is, "We're doing ok, why should we bother changing or even thinking about change?" A good example of this would be a value-added chain that offers a premium service (e.g. a hair and beauty salon) that is faced with a new competitor on the high street. The new competitor is offering much lower prices: how will the incumbent salon react? A common mistake is to engage in a price war, competing with the start-up on price. This will not prevent a loss of business and will erode the advantage the original company had in terms of service and quality. While a reactive approach will feel good to a manager who has only ever looked at the operational element of his business, this approach is not strategic.

A strategic response would be a campaign to existing clients emphasising the quality and premium nature of the service and trying to bond current clients on that basis.

- **A focus on 'cost' rather than 'value'**

Reliance on tight financial controls encourages decision-making consistent with short-term profit maximisation and risk avoidance. This can result in a lack of innovation and a loss of value. Innovation is what creates value and new market opportunities and thus enables organisations to operate more efficiently.

We've already looked at how the boss rose to his current position of authority, and the baggage this encumbers him with in terms of his ability, or lack of ability, to think strategically. Because of this history, the following issues can also contribute to a lack of strategic thinking:

Arrogance was examined in Chapter 1, together with the illusion of omni-competence, how we tend to be overly critical of any information that appears to contradict our present beliefs and how organisations can uncritically accept the way things get done.

Chapter 3 covered the fear of failure and the need to 'unlearn' what got the boss here. In addition to having to learn something new without any guarantee of success, there may also be a fear of committing to a target and of the boss being negatively perceived by his peers if this does not happen.

Finally, you may simply be dealing with an extreme alpha male who enjoys power and control whilst presiding over his minions. Any process that is perceived to threaten this position of power and control will, in all likelihood, decrease the degree of flexibility he has in making decisions and is therefore unlikely to be positively received.

We've spent a good deal of time talking about change. Jo has a big job on her hands, though, because change is often difficult and can meet with strong resistance. The details on how to move the culture and, indeed, the whole organisation, make up the second half of this book.

Let's start to examine this challenge in Chapter 5.

RESISTANCE TO CHANGE

THE CRUNCHY BIT

Resistance to change is almost inevitable. It's a natural human response to what is, after all, a perceived threat: what you already do and know feels safe, while anything new is less familiar and therefore feels less secure.

Change requires an effort. Even those of us who are most receptive to change need to be convinced of the need for it. You can try to overwhelm this resistance with brute force, or you could address yourself to reducing the resistance. Or both: if you understand why someone's reluctant to make a change, you can help to make the change easier for him while urging him on.

There are all sorts of justifications given for this resistance. If you'd like some detail on what you might encounter and why, have a look at the latter part of this chapter.

IT'S NOT MY IDEA SO I DON'T WANT TO DO IT

Jo's been thinking about Charlotte's story of the monkeys (see Chapter 1). In much the same way as the monkeys became used to 'how things are done around here', an organisation can become fixed in a pattern of work or response to a challenge that is no longer appropriate. It might be holding the organisation back. This can contribute to resistance to change.

You need to assess the impact of management practices and obstacles to engagement before attempting to arrive at a plan for a solution. We discussed this to some extent in Chapter 4. This work is important. It will help you to prioritise where you are going to focus most of your effort and it will allow you to benchmark where the company is right now. If you can repeat this at regular intervals, it will help you to determine how well your initiatives are bearing fruit.

As the Australian based academic psychologist and writer, Cordelia Fine, says in her 2007 book, *A Mind of its Own*, "evidence that supports your case is quickly accepted ... However, evidence that threatens [it] is subjected to gruelling cross-examination." This will, of course, apply to your boss. But it could also apply to those who are generally like-minded. They might have trouble accepting your perception of the problem and your suggested answers. Whilst they might like the general idea of change, they will defend their own patches for exactly the reasons the boss defends his: they were made in their image and change can imply imperfection. The best example of this was the way in which the suggestion that the earth was round, not flat, was greeted at the time. How many people were burnt at the stake, excommunicated or expelled from their communities before this heresy was accepted as fact? The whole world had to change its paradigm for this idea to be accepted –

and it did! That should give you heart as you face the challenge in your company.

Just bear in mind that this resistance to change might apply to you, too! Another reason why you need external sources like your survey to validate that what you perceive is a true reflection of reality.

In a recent experiment, a group of dogs was shown a number of potential routes from one side of a room to another and, if they made it across, there was a treat waiting for them. After even a single success, most dogs found it incredibly difficult to deal with any alteration in the successful pathway: they would always go back to the path that had given them success the first time, even though it had been blocked for the past attempts. In some cases it took weeks of retraining after a single successful foray for a dog to learn a new route.

In the same way, our preconceptions can often prove inadequate in the face of changed circumstances. Humans need time to break down or unlearn a strongly held belief, or conventional wisdom. This is difficult. It is difficult even if we consciously want to do it or are committed to change. Bear this in mind, especially when you meet severe resistance when attempting to help someone unlearn something they are not yet committed to changing.

A CONVENIENT TRUTH

Often 'truths' or accepted wisdoms develop within a person

or organisation and are uncritically accepted – as was the case with Charlotte's monkeys. When this happens, it becomes part of the normal system in that organisation or for that person. If the statements are *actually* true, their truth can be tested. However, if they are wrong, then by accepting them uncritically they add unnecessarily to the financial overheads of the organisations. For example, your organisation might be trying to manage work rotas for 2,500 staff in 200 locations on Excel spreadsheets instead of using specialised software. The cost of the software is cited as the reason not to change – ignoring the cost of the ten people currently doing the rotas (badly), or the misery their mistakes cause the employees. To attempt to do a management job on auto-pilot, so to speak, is really to reinforce the power of our preconceptions. Successful management does not just happen, it needs thinking about and working at.

You, like all managers, need to form your own opinions and not let received wisdom rule. Don't uncritically accept conventional wisdom, guard against:

- Wish fulfilment – accepting the 'wisdom' may feed an inner desire that has not yet been recognised or acknowledged. If you're growing your organisation because that gives you a sense of security, you risk doing so in spite of negative cash flow or other dangers.
- Fear – change should not be frightening, but judged against criteria of success or failure. Discomfort is a normal part of a change process. Recognise the discomfort, but embrace change for the better.

- Leaning on authority – no matter how reassuring! Also avoid using the 'power' conferred by authority to justify the *status quo*. For example, simply saying, "I am the manager and know what's best," is not a convincing argument.
- Rule-governed behaviour – where people adhere to rules irrespective of whether or not this truly serves the situation best. Back to the ten monkeys! If the water hose hasn't been used or even seen for weeks, should touching the ladder still be forbidden?
- Lack of interest or curiosity – intellectual curiosity is key to innovation and development.

Bear in mind that senior managers, too, are potential victims of the same phenomena and require some form of objective sounding board to test the validity and reliability of their observations and proposed solutions. In fact, there are numerous, well-documented studies showing that other people often assess our competence and prospects better than we do ourselves. Self-assessments are not just inaccurate; they tend to be flawed in a positive direction. Franklin Roosevelt is attributed with the quip, "the ablest man I ever met is the one you think you are." It appears that all of us have similarly immodest and unrealistic views of ourselves.

Most people tend to think of themselves as anything but average. They claim to be more disciplined, idealistic and socially skilled, and better at driving and leadership as well as being healthier than average. On average, we can't all be above average! We can't all be above average drivers

– can we? This is a mathematical impossibility. Nevertheless, many surveys show most people believing they excel among their contemporaries. Ironically, people also claim to be better than most at producing unbiased and realistic self-evaluations.

This can lead to poor decision-making, or the development of the faulty conventional wisdom previously mentioned. Poor performers tend not to be aware of just how badly they perform. This is probably because they lack the skills and expertise to recognise a correct decision. They may not recognise their own lack of self-awareness, and, as a consequence, believe they are doing just fine. In fact, they believe they are doing even better than most other people. We all know poor performers who think they are stars, totally oblivious to what the rest of the office thinks of them.

Don't underestimate the stamina required to turn any organisation onto a new course. When you have senior support and cooperation, change takes time – without support, it takes much longer. Setbacks will await and successes may be completely negated if your agenda is discovered.

How realistic are the changes you envisioned? Is the stretch too great? In other words, do you have small enough steps built into the process to ensure you generally only make forward movement? If you haven't, then you need to look at this very carefully before you even start considering 'selling' your dream to anyone else. Remember, at the early stages, especially if you have limited influence, it is very risky to accept a 'two steps forwards and one step backwards' philosophy: that step backwards might just be enough to precipitate your unplanned exit!

Resistance to change is your most significant obstacle.

ONLY TWO THINGS IN LIFE ARE CERTAIN: DEATH AND TAXES

To that we can add a third: change.

Despite the fact that much has been written on change and how one should embrace it, most of us spend our lives attempting to minimise the impact of change through planning, systems, processes and routines. More progressive managers attempt to overcome this fear consciously and actively embrace change. Their world view is that if change is going to happen, they should try to be at the leading edge. They see an opportunity in anticipating what needs to change before anyone else, thereby maintaining a competitive advantage. Some of the most adventurous see actually making changes happen as the way to go. If you recognise any people like that in your organisation, make friends quickly! They are just the sort you need to help you implement your plan.

There is, of course, another group who will only accept change when it is absolutely inevitable. An element of conservatism does have its benefits in avoiding rushing headlong into every new hare-brained scheme. It can be hugely frustrating, though, to watch someone metaphorically driving down the road towards a brick wall until they collide with it. Then, just to confirm that the wall is truly there, they back up and once again drive full speed into it. Only now does the driver look for ways around the wall, seemingly oblivious to the damage caused to his vehicle in the process, often justifying the damage as inevitable. Perhaps you had eight people working on the Excel spreadsheet rota – who weren't coping. So, to resolve the problem, you hired an extra two!

What makes matters worse is that the coping strategies they have developed in order to deal with a crisis have become entrenched into the standard way of doing things. Inefficiency becomes embedded into 'the way things get done around here'. A bit like the monkeys from Chapter 1, wouldn't you agree?

If this kind of strategy is repeated often enough, it leads the organisation to develop a unique approach when dealing with day-to-day issues. This 'uniqueness' then feeds on itself and gives substance to the belief that the organisation is different, reinforcing the *status quo* and effectively precluding change.

While resistance to change is at the heart of many of the problems facing you and the company, it may manifest itself in a variety of ways.

INADEQUATE OR ABSENT PLANNING

The boss might say, "If we were to spend all our time working out ways to deal with the infinite number of theoretical problems that could arise, we would not have enough time in the day to get the work done that actually needs doing. Planning is not a very efficient use of time because after we have put together a comprehensive and thorough plan, the future will present us with something which was not taken into consideration and our entire planning effort will have been a complete waste of time."

Brian is dead set against a business plan. He sees it as a waste of time and effort and as a purely theoretical exercise. Why try to say what you're going to do in the coming year or years when that will be so largely dictated by outside, unpredictable forces? Brian feels that forecasts or predictions, as set out in the business plan, are unlikely to materialise. The fact that a business plan, like a road map, can help him to plan for and better deal with those unforeseen eventualities is completely overlooked!

The essence of what we are dealing with here is the belief that a strong cadre of fire-fighters is a unique, efficient and differentiating core competence for the organisation!

LACK OF BENCHMARKING OR CLEAR GOAL-SETTING

Imagine what Brian might say: "We are very flexible and able to change and respond to situations as they arise. Sometimes an opportunity will present itself which, had we had a strong focus on a specific goal, we might have overlooked. It is important that we work hard at trying to be flexible, open and able to react to any new opportunities that might present themselves. Look at how successful we are without this theoretical stuff, let's just continue to do what we do well."

What might often be underlying this is the fear of a lack of control or the possibility of being judged badly by others when their aspirational goals are not met.

Another underlying issue could be the 'it's my train set and I'll play with it as I see fit.' While closely linked to the power issue, there's also a potential that involving others in 'his' game may result in him not being able to play with things in a way that he would like. After all, he does know best… just look at his track record. And that's a powerful argument to counter.

POOR STAFF MORALE AND RETENTION

The boss could say, "Our culture and our way of doing things are unique, and people are either with us or against us. The best way to find this out is to put them to the test: let them work for us. And, if they don't fit in, then we'll find a replacement. Most of the staff dissatisfaction stems from the fact that they don't fully understand the issues at stake here. If they would put themselves in my shoes, they would understand much better and be more compliant. Our sector is notorious for high staff turnover, and we don't have the funds to spend on motivational pep talks: we pay them to do a job so let them do it!"

He may have a truly internal focus with an inability to empathise with the staff. People need to understand *his* issues and if they would only take the time to understand what he was facing, then they would have more patience and tolerance.

DISEMPOWERED MANAGERIAL HIERARCHY

The boss might say, "Most people don't do things as well as I do. As they gradually become familiar with the way I do things, I can ease off giving them such detailed instructions, as I know they will be doing things in line with the way I think and would like. What I need is loyalty and people who will do what I want them to do in the way I would do it."

Managers within this culture are simply an extra pair of hands for the boss. By keeping power to himself, the boss makes himself indispensable, which feeds his feelings of power and authority, especially if a bottleneck develops that only he can resolve. Jo finds that she's not given the authority to make even the most basic decisions. She's found a great new supplier for SimianSynergy's inks and papers, but can't finalise the deal without Brian double-checking. Even though the products are clearly of better quality – and cheaper!

Managers must show deference and demonstrate that their values are closely aligned with the boss'. Jo's noticed that those of her colleagues who agree most loudly with Brian are given the most autonomy, albeit limited. There is likely to be no significant devolution of power or development of real middle management competencies. Those privileged enough to enjoy a position of power tend to use it to serve their own ends with a negative impact on the rest of the team. It is obviously not in the interests of the boss' henchmen, the Powerful Others, to encourage any true forms of management development or empowerment as this is likely to negatively affect their position and status. In fact, they may even feed disinformation to the boss in order to justify their positions and entrench channels of communication to the boss through them. For example, a Powerful Other team leader may have risen to a position where his status and role cannot be questioned. This may be in spite of the fact that he is making no significant contributions to the team output. To protect his position, he may regale the boss with tales of his own cleverness, loyalty and cunning, demonstrating his indispensability.

TEAM-BUILDING DEFICITS

The boss might say, "Things are good. I am delivering value to the shareholders and the organisation. Those who oppose what I'm doing have no part in the organisation. We need people who are like-minded, not those whose egos stop the company delivering value and profit. There are plenty of people I consult with and they say I'm doing a great job!"

He might feel that, as long as the organisation performs financially, there is nothing to worry about. He believes the problem is other people, who need to be educated to bring them into line. If that's not possible, then he'd rather they left. A less extreme example would be the boss who sees what needs to be done to a degree but is just not very good at making it happen – especially if he is in fire-fighting mode. SimianSynergy is making good money. Brian may be aware that staff turnover is high, but he's reluctant to make changes in spite of the high indirect costs of staff replacement.

PROBLEMS AND AGENDAS AMONG SENIOR MANAGERS

Many projects involving teams can suffer from a lack of common vision or strategy. This may or may not be apparent. Multidisciplinary teams assembled on the basis of perceived required skill sets may have complementary technical skills but lack the social or emotional ability to complement one another in order to achieve optimal project completion. Simian's accountant might be a necessary part of the team working on a new project, but can he support the creative designers and copywriters? Poor fit can be due to differences in cultural backgrounds, past experience and even world views. All too often these differences are subtle enough to prevent a common vision from forming. Whilst subtle differences may appear insignificant, the potential to affect the implementation of projects should not be overlooked. Variety is certainly the spice of life, and having different viewpoints can enrich a project. But be mindful that this variety can also cause tensions on a team.

The success of most projects depends on a blend of technical, personnel and conceptual skills. The relationship between these and the emphasis placed on each will depend on which level the team is operating. Nevertheless, these skills manifest in some form of behaviour or other. Impacting on this are knowledge and value systems.

In a similar way the progress and, indeed, success of many projects reflects the interaction between the task and variables attributable to the team and/or the individual. Sadly, the appointment of people to many projects relies predominantly on technical competence and neglects these factors – which we accept can be hard to measure. Often a track record may provide convincing evidence of potential performance. While it can certainly be a guide to future performance, past success in one, two or more teams in no way guarantees future success in other teams – or even in the same team under different circumstances! There are methods to avoid this, but these are beyond the scope of this text.

It makes sense to attempt to maximise the potential for success where projects have reached the stage of funding, resource allocation and other support. Gaps in conceptual, interpersonal and technical skills should be identified early and remedial action taken. The early integration of each member into the team, as well as the development of team spirit, is a recognised method of enhancing performance and reducing conflict. To this end, it is key to have a well formulated and agreed upon strategic focus, as well as an implementation plan, and to monitor progress closely. You may or may not have the direct authority to do this, but be aware of the need for these and draw attention to any problems that arise.

The unique nature of each individual, each team and consequently each project, necessitates a tailor-made approach in order to have the best chance of success.

Jerry has had personal experience of this. He used to work for a generic pharmaceutical company that was the market leader in a specific medical niche.

The company had built its reputation in the industry for adhering to the highest standards in manufacturing and quality control. For years it followed the same procedures and prospered despite strong competition. Suddenly, in the space of a few months, sales dropped dramatically. The management frantically tried to figure out what was going wrong. Each part of the leadership team pointed the finger at another. The Managing Director blamed the production department, the Production Manager blamed the pricing structure, the Finance Director blamed marketing, and the Marketing Manager blamed a lack of sales resource!

There was no team analysis of what the competition was doing – in fact, quite the opposite! Some departments and groups had some market intelligence but a co-ordinated, integrated perspective was lacking. Each group was looking at only its piece of the jigsaw puzzle and was communicating primarily from that perspective. The result: a continued and worsening slump that finally drove Jerry to leave!

AN OVERRIDING AND UNSUSTAINABLE PROFIT IMPERATIVE

The boss might say, "We don't have the money to spend on the niceties of looking after the staff. They are paid to do a job and offering them incentives or giving them additional perks will simply erode our profitability. If they do a good job, we will be able to continue to grow and increase performance, and then the benefits will be there for everyone to enjoy. We are running a business and if we did what everyone wanted or thought was a good idea, we would have no profits left. Our job is not to win popularity contests with our staff." Happily, this viewpoint is in a fast-shrinking minority!

Internal consistency is important: if your organisation buys the cheapest stock it can and then tries to sell it on as a 'value' item, that can create internal tensions. If, for example, that inconsistency adversely affects the sales team, they will be forced either to lie to their clients or to leave.

HIDDEN AGENDAS

We all know that most of communication is non-verbal, highlighting the importance of body language. An underlying mismatch between what management say they want and their underlying aim is likely to cause problems. It has also never been more prone to exposure than in the 21st century. Whilst the more traditional routes continue to play a vital role in communication, we are also faced with a cornucopia of electronic media through which the world can be reached by a single individual. That means that the mismatch mentioned above is bound to be spotted – sooner rather than later. For example, in Simian's case, the organisation should be aligned around providing great customer service. If Brian's real agenda is to maximise profits by cutting all costs to the bone, that will create an internal tension that can't be addressed directly because it's hidden from the management and staff.

Never has it been more vital to ensure that your organisational ethos really matches the values you have as the manager or leader. In the past this lack of alignment could more easily be hidden because most advertising or marketing communication tended to be one-way, and word-of-mouth about the real values took time to gain traction. Before Facebook and the Internet, companies could advertise great quality of service. One to one word-of-mouth about their actual, poor service may have had an effect but this would have been restricted to the disgruntled customer's limited social circle. Today, one unhappy customer can (and does!) speak to the world.

There needs to be clear alignment and synchronicity of values. This is essential, from the recruitment of people, through to service delivery. Any mismatch is likely to be picked up by team members and this will impact on the customer experience. Not only that, but email, Twitter,

Facebook and other social media or even text message word-of-mouth, both positive and negative, will affect your business far quicker than it ever did in the past. It is important to understand that this cannot simply be controlled or managed away. You should define clearly what the organisation's core values are and then live them. Even if the motive is profit, this needs to be driven by an offer that is related to a value system. Do this and the profits will follow. If this is not the case, you are unlikely to succeed at developing a sustainable business model.

FINALLY(!): OMNIPOTENT CONSERVATISM AND FEAR OF CHANGE

It is likely to be even more pronounced and problematical if the boss has a very dominant and controlling personality or social style.

Charlotte is round for dinner with Jo and Jerry and conversation has moved from the difficulties of finding good decorators to Jo's challenges at work. Jo's convinced that understanding Simian's resistance to change is the final key in the puzzle. With this information she is certain that she now knows how to fix any blockages and unleash the true potential of the organisation.

"You know, Jo-Jo, you're right about resistance," says Jerry. "But, tell me, how do you know what Simian's potential is?"

"What do you mean?"

"Well, all companies have people with varying abilities, and equipment that may or may not be used to its full potential. If you know what the potential is, you can judge whether or not it's worth the effort you'll have to put in.

"If Simian has the potential to be the great company you think it can be, then it's probably worth considering making the effort. But if it can only improve a little, there's little point in killing yourself because the company simply doesn't have the potential to be great. Does that make sense?"

"Not really," Jo says. "I'm not really with you."

"Well, you love your art. If you owned a dirty old oil painting that needed cleaning, how much would you reasonably pay for cleaning and restoration? If it was an old master you'd be willing to pay a fortune. But if it was one of mine, I think you'd use an old rag for five minutes at most! The same applies to how much effort you're willing to expend on Simian."

Jo is silent for a while, thinking carefully. "You're right," she says, finally. "I'd better check or I'll just set myself up for disappointment.

"Charlie, can I get that painter's number? I really need to get the bedroom repainted."

Right, let's move on to look at the potential of the organisation in Chapter 6.

6
ASSESSING THE ORGANISATION'S POTENTIAL

THE CRUNCHY BIT

You really can't make a silk purse from a sow's ear.

What you're setting out to achieve will, as you've already gathered, require a lot of effort. There is absolutely no point in expending any energy at all, however, if the raw materials you have to work with are not capable of achieving what you envisage.

So, how do you evaluate your organisation's potential? You could use key texts (Jim Collins' Good to Great, *for example) to see how far you are from his ideal and whether your organisation has the ability to get there. Or you could look for a unique approach or skill set in your organisation: even without any* Good to Great *characteristics, if you've got something unique to work with, it may be worth making the effort. And, if you find neither a competitive advantage nor one of Collins' criteria, you might want to think very carefully before pouring your energies into this project.*

The song has it that the thigh bone's connected to the knee bone. Organisations are heavily connected entities, and changing one aspect will almost certainly have an effect on another. That effect may not be anticipated! The better you know the structure and links within your organisation, the more you'll be able to anticipate how your changes may play out – and which levers should be pulled and which should be left well alone.

We've looked at your frustrations, what type of boss and organisation you have and how the organisation developed into what you see today. We've also looked at the resistance you're likely to encounter.

Making change happen is hard work. Why would you bother if it isn't going to be change for the better? And that sort of change requires you to think big, REALLY BIG.

GOOD, OR GREAT?

In his seminal work, *Good to Great,* Jim Collins goes into great detail on many of these ideas. The concepts he identifies are important and we've summarised them for you here. (Copyright © 2001 Reprinted by permission of Curtis Brown, Ltd) In a nutshell, he says that great companies all share five fundamental characteristics.

Collins' book takes as its starting point companies that have achieved great results for a sustained period and then rigorously investigates why these results were achieved. It makes sense, therefore, to use his list as a set of aspirational targets for your organisation.

1: LEADERSHIP
Leaders of the great companies are ambitious, but their

ambition is first and foremost for the organisation and not for themselves.

2: CLARITY OF PURPOSE

Whilst numerous textbooks have been written on this subject, Collins' research shows that great organisations have absolute clarity of purpose and understanding on the following three issues:

- What they could excel at (ideally 'best in the world') i.e. they were sure of exactly what they could do fantastically well and were equally aware of what they couldn't
- Exactly what drove their economic engine i.e. how to generate a sustained and robust cash flow and profitability most effectively
- Which activities they were deeply passionate about.

The simultaneous presence of *all three* themes distinguished the great from the good. Don't be put off by this! Collins' study shows that, on average, it took four years of sustained effort for companies to get to this point. Whilst getting there is important, the process by which companies got there was equally important. This is all about the ability to face reality.

3: CULTURE OF DISCIPLE

Companies need to face reality. As Collins says, when "… *you start with an honest and diligent effort to determine the truth of the situation, the right decisions often become self-evident.*" It is important to create a culture that allows the truth to be aired. To some extent you can spend less time and energy motivating the right people if they are self-starters. What you do need to do is create an environment that does not *de*motivate them. To do this, Collins suggests embedding the following practices into the culture of the team:

- Focus on **questions** to try to fully understand problems or issues (ask the questions that will lead to the team sharing their insights)
- Engage in **dialogue and debate**, not in coercion (involve people in uncovering the solutions to their problems)
- Conduct autopsies **without blame** (the issue is learning and understanding to prevent future recurrences rather than looking for a scapegoat)
- Build **early warning systems** for system or process failures (the difference between the good and great companies was not more or better information systems, but the way in which the information was processed and presented – especially when the company could not afford to ignore it!).

This may seem like just another list of things to do, but it's important to **begin with the end in mind**. We're sure that's been mentioned before!

We're not expecting these systems to be present in your organisation right now. But you do need to assess the boss and the team for the potential to develop an alternative culture. Of all the criteria we have mentioned so far, this one has the greatest potential to effect change by carefully and consistently nudging people in the right direction. In terms of perspective, it is essential to test your perceptions of reality with others. Are others in agreement with you regarding the situation? You might want some independent verification: from exit interviews, for example.

4: APPROPRIATE USE OF TECHNOLOGY

In the 21st century, change as a result of technology is commonplace. However, what distinguishes great companies from good companies is their perspective on the appropriate use of technology. When used appropriately, technology facilitates the development of momentum rather than creating it i.e. it facilitates forward movement, rather than being the driver of that movement. Until you are clear as to why the technology is relevant, you are unlikely to be using it at its optimal potential. In fact, Collins' study shows using exactly the same leading technologies would not have helped great companies' competitors to raise their game to the same level! Technology served the companies because they were set up to make best use of it.

If the team or the boss is addicted to technology as the solution to the problems or the 'way forward', you might be well advised to reconsider taking on this challenge.

5: ACTIONS ALIGNED AROUND A COMMON PURPOSE

Success comes through the cumulative effects of clearly understood actions aligned around a common purpose. Collins clearly shows that many or most of the apparent overnight successes of great companies were as a result of years of hard work to start the ball rolling. Then, as it gained momentum, more work was required to keep it rolling in the right direction.

Now we need to turn to the organisation's potential: is it able to transcend mediocrity? In other words, if you are successful in your mission of converting people to your cause, to what extent are the building blocks for change already there? In order to find this out, you need to perform an 'inventory check'. An inventory check is, effectively, a list on which you identify those factors which the organisation will need in order to be great, compared to what it actually has. The inventory check can also be used as a tool in forming your plan, as we described earlier. It allows an accurate assessment of the status quo and, with that, you can plan more realistically for the future.

That's all great, thank you Mr Collins, but not only do you need to know what you have at your disposal, you also need to be able to assess whether or not you can use these resources effectively to achieve your ultimate goal.

Things to check would include:

- Competitive advantage
- Strategic plan
- Underlying culture

You may believe your company has the potential to make a significant difference in the market. And you may feel it has the potential to sustain this competitive advantage. But does the organisation have any competitive advantage? Does it have the potential to develop this?

Here is a framework that may help you understand whether your view of things is accurate or not:

YET ANOTHER CHECKLIST

1: Competitive advantage, in simple terms, refers to those things that the company does better or more efficiently than anyone else. It's what gives a company its edge.

Competitive advantage is determined or limited by the organisation's capabilities, and can roughly be divided into 'distinctive' and 'reproducible' capabilities.

Distinctive capabilities are those unlikely to be replicated by competitors – or only with extreme difficulty e.g. government licences, patents or copyrights. However, things such as strong branding, a specific type of customer relationship or even skills, knowledge and routines could play a role. Steve Jobs developed a distinctive capability for his Apple brand by creating or perfecting the user interface and experience with his devices. SimianSynergy, like most (all?) creative agencies, uses only Apple products. From this user experience grew an almost obsessive Apple fan base with enormous brand loyalty. The brand became, in effect, its own distinctive capability: if it was Apple it was good and if it wasn't, well, it wasn't.

Facebook, for all of its early years, had distinctive capabilities in the way personal data was stored and shared. By the time competitors matched these original capabilities, Facebook had such a weight of users that its size became another distinctive capability: it connected more people than any other social networking site.

Reproducible capabilities are more easily bought,

created or copied, provided the competitor has adequate skills, diligence and financial resources. As we've already mentioned about Facebook, above, it has a huge head start on other social networks. If, however, a giant competitor like Google was willing to invest enough money and time in competing with them, with a bit of luck, it might match or even exceed Facebook's advantages. Bear in mind that, in most cases, it is **distinctive** capabilities that form the basis of sustained competitive advantage. If Google+ can match Facebook's user base, that size will stop being a distinctive capability for Facebook and make it less likely that Facebook would be the first choice of a new user joining a social network. There's just as good a chance that a new user's friends and colleagues might now be on the Google+ network as being on Facebook.

To assess the true potential of your organisation, you must consider what its distinctive capabilities are. In addition to these distinctive, unique attributes, other advantages are very useful. These **reproducible** capabilities include good working conditions or talented staff. You need these reproducible qualities in order to take advantage of those that are distinctive: to market them effectively, to get the best from them or to attract more great staff members. You also must consider in which markets this can give you an overall competitive advantage.

To sum up: your organisation's competitive advantage is the sum of its key distinctive capabilities and its supporting, reproducible capabilities. In most cases, both subcategories are needed.

2: To help with your inventory analysis, it is worth defining the business in terms of its **strategic plan** – even in the absence of a mission statement. If a mission statement does exist, start with this and work towards a vision from which a business strategy should emerge. This then should culminate in a business plan as discussed in Chapter 4.

It really doesn't matter what shape this plan takes as long as there is some kind of strategic thinking. Whether the plan is a back of the envelope sketch, a balanced scorecard analysis or a formal annual business plan, the fact that it exists at all is useful. If the plan does exist, even in outline, you need to evaluate it critically to determine to what extent it needs to be modified to move the business in the direction you think best. We will be looking at concrete examples of how to do this in due course. You may need to devise a road map that will facilitate the process of making the required changes, as we previously explained.

If there is no plan, you need to try to deduce what the boss and the Powerful Others think this should be. You should at the very least be able to infer a vision or a mission from them, and then decide whether this is adequate to take the organisation where it needs to go. Even if their plan seems misguided, it still gives you a starting point in your inventory analysis. For example, if their agenda is all about profit and control, their strategic plan may well be to continue to drive cash flow and profitability above all else and to remain in direct control of operations. This 'plan', while it exists in their minds, may be grossly inadequate, but at least it gives you a starting point to work from.

The parameters mentioned so far are traditionally called 'hard' and tend to be easier to influence or change –

so why are we putting so much store on them? This is because the business plan sets the path that the organisation intends to follow and you need to know what the current trajectory is in order to recalibrate and aim for something different! The reason these are (relatively) easy to change is that it's a fairly simple matter to write a new mission statement or refine a business plan. Changing a culture is much more difficult...

3: A company's **underlying culture**, values and ethos underpin the mission and plan. They are also more difficult to influence directly and will either enhance or hinder the achievement of the hard targets. If your organisation has relatively clearly defined hard targets, you need to examine whether the real values, ethos and culture match what's written down. Do the workers believe in what the boss says they believe in? If not, then something is wrong. If you agree with the hard issues, then the solution lies in developing processes and systems that will encourage the staff to live, eat and breathe these values, at least while they're at work! If there is a mismatch and you don't think the mission statement is correct, then we suggest you start over. This time create a mission statement that reflects the values, ethos and culture of the organisation as it is, or one that allows you realistically to mould the ethos to your way of thinking. The authors took part in an exercise within their own company in which the directors held a facilitated workshop to help them refocus and reappraise their company's mission and vision. The organisation wanted to ensure that it was fully aligned with the caring, skilled and dedicated staff that it employed. The result of this was to create a fresh vision for the company, embodied in the call to action, 'Be amazing'.

Whilst all this may seem like a rather academic exercise at this stage, it is highly advisable that you spend time exploring the match between the plan and the underlying values and culture thoroughly. To paraphrase Jerry's words to Jo at the end of the last chapter, you don't want to commit significant time and energy in training a dinosaur only to find that it is shortly to become extinct!

Perhaps there is only a single, dominant issue. On the other hand, many of the considerations outlined above are inter-related and it is not uncommon to find that you are confronted with the need to significantly restructure the organisation on multiple fronts, especially from a cultural point of view.

As we mentioned in Chapter 4, you need a plan of action: what are you going to achieve for your company? The organisation itself, on the other hand, may only develop a formal business plan late in its evolution. To help you understand why this is likely to be the case, we would like to propose a model for looking at the 'big picture'.

A BUSINESS IS VERY MUCH LIKE A JENGA® TOWER

Businesses are made up of large numbers of parts which, together, make up a solid and stable structure. Whilst we accept that often issues are interrelated and interdependent, for the purposes of this model, let's just assume that one can clearly separate their inter-relatedness and settle purely for interdependence.

To build a strong tower that is stable and has the potential to grow in height through the addition of new blocks, we need ALL the blocks in the existing tower to be securely in place. It's possible to remove a few blocks without substantially affecting the stability of the tower, but you can't remove too many! In fact, if you continue to remove block after block, the basic stability of the existing tower becomes threatened.

In the same way, your organisation can probably cope with, for example, a poor management infrastructure but, as the number of substandard departments becomes more numerous, the overall stability of your organisation becomes threatened. Growth is still possible but a shaky foundation makes the process more perilous.

A further useful insight that this model provides is in how many ways things can go wrong. If the tower is relatively stable and we introduce a weakness into the system by removing a block, this is unlikely to result in its collapse. However, if a number of other blocks are already missing and the tower is becoming inherently unstable, the removal of the 'staff motivation' block may result in the collapse of the tower.

When this happens, the collapse is often perceived to be principally resulting from the removal of that particular block rather than as a result of the overall instability of the entire tower. Consequently, the overall organisational effort is primarily focused on the offending 'block' rather than on understanding that, had the other 'blocks' been in place, the removal of the single extra one might only have contributed to some minor instability.

In the authors' field of veterinary medicine, clients will often ask why their dog or cat got sick. The answer is never simple: because it got a virus, for example. There are always a number of factors at work: the animal's diet might have been sub-optimal, it may have got cold and wet for a long period, there may have been a new animal in the house that was causing stress and anxiety. If it was exposed to a virus on top of all these other factors, its immune system wasn't able to cope and it got sick. If none of the other factors had been present there is every chance that the dog would simply have shrugged off the virus and the owner would never have needed to ask the question about why it got sick!

In the same way, there will probably not be a single cause for the problems at your organisation, or Jo's. All

The Jenga® Model – don't remove too many bricks...

sorts of factors will add to each other to give rise to the complex web of challenges you and she currently face.

This perspective is helpful in understanding the interdependence of the various factors and the importance of addressing the sum of the parts in order to achieve a successful, stable whole.

In looking at how things interrelate, it's quite likely that you will find things you were not looking for. If you want your workplace Jenga® tower to be solid and stable, these new issues will require the same time and energy as the issues that first came to your attention and inspired you to pick up this book. Jo, for example, finds that the copy department performs very poorly. As she investigates this, she realises that the reason for poor performance in that department is bullying. She didn't expect to find bullying but, now that she has, she needs to deal with it.

The morning after having Charlotte round for dinner, Jerry and Jo are chatting over cups of hangover coffee.

"Jo, I'm a bit worried about you," Jerry says. "You've looked at why you're frustrated, Simian's background and why it's resistant to change as well as Brian's strengths and weaknesses and those of your colleagues. "But what about you? I know you can do pretty much anything you set your mind to, including learning new skills or ways of working. What do you think you'll need to learn in order to make the changes you want at Simian?"

Jerry's right, but there's even more to this than what he's

mentioned. For example, does Jo have the patience needed, or the resilience to accept setbacks and keep trying, and can she deal with conflict? In short, can she sustain her levels of motivation to see the project through? We'll look at some aspects of this in the next chapter.

7
YOUR ABILITIES AND RESOURCES

THE CRUNCHY BIT

Do you have the skills and ability to take this project forward? How can you tell?

Middle managers are critical in managing change. The most important step is to identify an end point. With that destination in mind, you are in a position to plot your route, step by step, from where you are now to where you want to be. With a destination in mind, you'll be able to judge how far you've come and how much further there is to go. This will be very useful in reassuring you that progress really is made – a little like looking back at the view when you're climbing a steep hill. There may be far to go, but just look how far you've come!

Before you set off, have you checked that your assumptions about where you are now, and the feasibility of your end point, are correct? And at what stage of preparedness for change are your potential allies?

In order to evaluate that readiness for change, you'll need to be an accurate judge of your people. Situational Leadership II skills are particularly helpful if you want to be able to support each of your team in the way that they need. You'll need to be inspirational

– by coaching and mentoring people, for example. (Don't forget to get your own coaching, too!) You'll need to be assertive without being aggressive. And you'll need to be able to interpret the feedback you receive accurately: is the person who usually argues with you a supporter or opponent of the changes you propose? Is he obstructing you, or is he actually engaging with your proposals, examining them and trying to find a fit?

You may find allies in unlikely places. Just because someone works outside your organisation doesn't mean he can't help or support you.

The most important agent of change for your organisation is YOU. If you need extra help or coaching to elevate your skills to the required level, don't be afraid to seek it.

CAN WE DO IT? YES WE CAN!

What follows in this chapter is a look at what you'll need to do to effect change in your organisation, and how you might start going about it. Your task as you read on is to measure your own abilities against the task at hand. How well are you able to do what's being set out here? Do you need to enhance or develop your own abilities?

Your role as a manager is a vitally important one. Let's look at the value of the manager in making sense of change, implementing that change, and conveying its importance to the rest of the team.

The Advanced Institute of Management Research (AIM) provides some valuable insight into the challenges of managing the change process. In particular, AIM recognised the increasing importance of middle managers and how, in the absence of real clarity of purpose from the leadership, they become responsible for implementing changes whilst ensuring that day-to-day business continues. Additionally, AIM doubts the extent of influence that senior management can have in managing change – especially in larger, geographically dispersed, modular organisations. Finally, AIM states that "if senior management want to exert an influence … it needs to pay more attention to the lateral processes that middle managers engage in … peer interactions, for example."

To help you to evaluate your options realistically, you have assessed the organisation's potential, including the informal culture and staff goodwill. You are now ready to consider how influential you can be in your current position. Managing the boss will be just one part of the problem. To succeed, you will need to develop a critical mass of opinion to reach a tipping point. Remember, while you can try and ensure that most of your activities are aligned with this goal, you still have to do your day job! You need to consider what your present remit is and gauge the extent to which you can align most of your activities with achieving your vision for the team. Most of your actions should be aligned with the values and beliefs you consider necessary to move things forward. You need to "*begin with the end in mind*", as Stephen Covey puts it so well in *The 7 Habits of Highly Effective People*. Guard against being drawn off course.

The bullying that Jo uncovered in Chapter 6, for example, can be dealt with in a number of ways. Brian would simply storm in and put the bully in her place with a good telling off and a final warning, to boot. In terms of team effectiveness, the issue does need to be dealt with, but part of the solution might be to empower the bullied worker. This empowerment might prevent bullying from arising at all in the future.

This will also fit with your vision for the organisation: empowerment and self-reliance.

EVERYONE'S A CUSTOMER

You need to spend significant time selling not only your competencies, but your vision for the future. Anybody that you are selling your ideas to is, in effect, your potential customer. To sell these ideas effectively, your first step must be to understand that customer's perspective, their point of view.

You may find that there is resistance to your ideas, especially at first. Try to see opposition as a sign of engagement. Opponents need to think about what you're saying in order to disagree with it, and thinking about it signals involvement.

Assertiveness is an additional skill that may be useful here (it's useful elsewhere, too!).

To be more assertive, you need to:

- talk in terms of 'I'
- know what you want, be brief and get directly to the point

- express both positive and negative feelings
- say no without feeling guilty
- stand up for yourself and your rights.

We find The Forum Corporation's sales model useful as a tool for disseminating ideas about change through the organisation. The focus of their sales process is on relationships, not transactions. It's not about winning or losing a sale, it's about focusing on the customer, understanding his or her needs and helping them to make the right decision. In their model, the sale is the natural outcome of the relationship IF the company has the right product for that customer. If not, the relationship is strong enough for the salesperson to guide the customer to another product – and actually enhance their relationship in the process.

You need to employ fundamental selling skills consistently in order to move the sale of your ideas towards a close. Giving information and stating benefits is just one of the tools you would use to move people from a level of low interest to one of conviction or even commitment to your product, your cause. The degree to which you disclose your plan to others should be proportional to the level of interest shown. Temper your enthusiasm with judgement. Your approach should always be to question, listen and seek to understand what's going on in the minds of your potential allies and what their needs are.

NETWORKING

You need to know who you can sell to! In the words of John Donne: *"no man is an island, entire of itself…"* This is true of large organisations, too. We wholeheartedly concur with management writer Daniel Priestley's perspective that, today, networks are vital to the success of any person or organisation. These networks might be within your organisation but could just as easily be outside it. The networks might be people you know ('real') or those you're connected to in the online world, via LinkedIn or Facebook ('virtual'). Never underestimate the degree of influence a client, supplier or even a competitor may have! Given that you are looking at an approach incorporating gradual movement towards your goal, there may be times when all you might need to help your boss to take the next step is:

- a slightly stronger external nudge
- or a subtle change to the playing field
- or a change in the relationship dynamic
- or a carefully crafted, timed and placed message.

Your sales target check is now complete, and you've decided to proceed with your challenge – to turn the organisation onto the right path.

We can divide the feelings of your potential allies into five levels of interest. We highly recommend using The Forum Corporation's method of grouping all potential supporters or opponents into a category of interest, and starting to convert those who are closest to your goal first. The more success you have early on, even if only moral victories, the more others will take note.

The five levels of interest are:

1) Totally uninterested
2) Low interest
3) Strong interest
4) Convinced, but not yet committed
5) Committed

Opposition is a sign of interest! For someone to challenge your thinking or ideas, they have to have thought about them first. Even if it's a knee-jerk reaction, something has happened to trigger that response and gain their attention. You have an opportunity to engage with them, and that's at least at level two! Do not be put off by opposition. Also consider the extent to which you wish to make your agenda public.

First, try to identify which level people occupy, then apply the appropriate techniques to move them up the ladder until they are totally committed to your suggestions. They can then become advocates for your ideas. Appropriate questioning can help to show you the level of interest of your potential customers.

For example, Jo might ask a colleague, "What did you think of how Brian did that?" or, "What have you found works well in these situations? I've got some articles and a few books that talk about this problem – would you like to see them?" Depending on the colleague's response, Jo should be able to categorise their level of interest.

TOTAL UNINTEREST

Do not start with this cohort! As your agenda starts to gain traction, levels of interest will rise. Should someone in this group challenge your agenda, it should prompt you to re-examine the category you've put that person into: they're clearly interested enough to be asking questions! Don't forget that opposition is a sign of engagement. You'll identify this group by their behaviour and the support they give to the *status quo*. Could the Powerful Others fit into this group?

LOW INTEREST

To move this person to the next level requires very careful attention to detail and a significant time commitment. If you know what their needs are, you will have a better idea of how you can make them more interested in the solution to their (and your) problem.

> Brian had to deal with the bullying issue in the copy department, but it's recurred. He's very frustrated. "I've told Mel to stop picking on Sarah, but it's because she's such a flower. She's asking for it! Now I need to go and speak to Mel again when it's really Sarah who should be told off. What a pain!"

In this example, Brian isn't actually asking for help, but he's sharing frustration that he hasn't been able to resolve the issue. He's not a prime target, but he's at least somewhat open to discussion. This is a low level of interest.

The needs of those with low interest will primarily relate to either increasing or decreasing something:

i)   increasing – e.g. performance or output, status or salary
ii) decreasing – e.g. the level of staff turnover or, in Brian's case, Sarah's complaints about bullying.

If you cannot express their needs in terms of increases or decreases, it helps to get them to visualise clearly where they are now and where they'd like to be, especially if you are leading them to your preferred solution or vision. Your role is to help them clearly identify and visualise the gap between these states. The more you can exaggerate the gulf, the more they'll be interested in your solutions. For example, Jo could talk to Brian. The more frustrated she can make Brian with the *status quo*, the more likely it is that he'll listen to her advice. What Jo needs to do is to show Brian the gap between the *status quo* of low-level bullying in the copy department and the drain that creates on his time and energy, and the promised land of being able to ignore the copy team. If she can enlarge this gap, making the present situation seem even worse (highlighting how often he's being called out) and the desired outcome even better (Brian being left to concentrate on other things), the more Brian's interest will be pricked.

It's very important not to ask outright challenging or threatening questions, and to encourage and confirm their ideas liberally – especially where you've led them to the answers you were looking for. The higher value the questions you use (i.e. the more the person has to think about and formulate the answer), the more value the answer will hold for them. For example, if Jo were to ask Brian what he wanted to do about the problem in copy, that would be a low value question with a simple answer. Asking him how he feels about it, or what he thinks he could do differently to resolve it, is much more difficult for Brian to answer and of much higher value. "Well, Brian, shouting at Mel doesn't seem to have helped," Jo might say, "what else do you think you could do?"

You need to help Brian, or anyone else, understand what the consequences are if they do not follow their own suggestions. Make them aware of the benefits of moving to their own solutions and make them aware of the options they have to fulfil their needs.

People will much more readily believe the things that they have said themselves, rather than what they are told. Do your very best not to present solutions to the problem – let the person come to it by him or herself.

STRONG INTEREST

At this level your objective is to help people see solutions to the problem. Remember to speak of benefits.

Brian is busy considering Jo's question. What would he

do differently? He's come up with a couple of scenarios and has gone to find Jo to tell her what he's decided. Although he presents this as a 'decision', Jo recognises that Brian is, in fact, asking her opinion and wanting her feedback. If he was truly convinced he'd just go ahead and deal with Mel and Sarah. By coming to find Jo, Brian is indicating strong interest, even if he isn't willing to say so!

Brian is just one personality type. A less Results Rupert-like boss might simply ask for your opinion. That would be a sign of strong interest, too.

CONVINCED, BUT NOT YET COMMITTED

Recommend a course of action and encourage them to make a decision regarding it. Start with these people if you can!

Brian has now gone off to try a new tack with Mel and Sarah. He's come back to Jo delighted: what he discussed with Jo really worked! There does seem to be value in what she said.

If Jo's not careful, she'll try to push too hard. For example, she might want to set up a staff empowerment scheme or something similar. She needs to be careful because, while Brian is currently convinced by the results, he's not yet fully committed to the idea of employee empowerment.

That will still take some time and he'll need to see sustained results.

COMMITTED

Fully on board and ready to help. Your fully-formed ally.

It's a month or two later, and Brian hasn't been called back to the copy department. He's also used Jo's technique in the sales department where a similar problem occurred, with similarly good results. Jo asks him if he's pleased with the results and how much extra time he now has. He certainly is!

"Great," she says, "how do you want to roll this out across Simian?"

This presumptive close (the question makes the presumption that Brian does want to roll it out!) encourages Brian to take that final step. In so doing, he moves from being convinced to being fully committed. He can see the benefits and wants to embed them in the company.

Your organisation may have the potential to be great, but do you have the influence to make all the changes you think are needed in order to achieve greatness? What critical success factors are missing? A lack of business planning can be addressed fairly easily. But if you have ambitions to move the organisation beyond the here and now you will also need to have the business and strategic skills to make it happen. Do you have them, and if not, do you know someone who does? Will they help you?

Knowing what the basic requirements are for success is critical, and identifying how well your organisation is placed to deliver success is key to your future plans. It's no good investing a huge amount of time and effort in something that simply isn't going to happen. Taking stock is important.

EVEN THE LONGEST JOURNEY STARTS WITH A SINGLE STEP

While change is, indeed, a journey, a common mistake is to focus too much on the end vision and not enough on the first few steps.

During the course of this book we outline a process to follow that should help you achieve your ultimate aim. To sum it up in one short phrase, you need to *"begin with the end in mind"* (Stephen Covey, *The 7 Habits of Highly Effective People*). Once you have a clear focus on where you want the organisation and your supporters to be, you need to look for the appropriate moments to consistently and convincingly nudge it and them in that direction. A very effective technique to achieve this is called successive approximation.

Jo knows Charlotte's story about successive approximation very well. So well that she often tells it herself! It's about how lion tamers teach lions to jump through hoops.

The technique involves breaking the trick into a small number of easily achievable steps. Each is only slightly more complex than the preceding one and the lion is rewarded for appropriate behaviour as the task progresses.

The tamer starts with a specific spot in the arena and rewards the lion every time he moves to the spot when instructed. Once there is a strong and definite association between the reward and the correct behaviour, the tamer adds another small nuance to the process. For example, he might add a block only one step in height but large enough to easily accommodate the lion. The reward is now given only if the lion walks up to the spot and steps onto the block.

Depending on what the tamer wants to achieve, the next step may involve increasing the number of steps or raising the height of the platform – and again rewarding the lion when he displays the appropriate behaviour by stepping onto it. Once this is firmly embedded, he then places another platform adjacent to the first one. Now the lion is only rewarded when he walks from the first platform onto the second. Little by little, the distance between the two platforms is increased until the lion will walk up the steps onto the first platform and jump across an open space – landing on the second platform.

All that remains is to hold a hoop between the platforms and the training is complete!

In our example, Jo has kept her eye firmly on her goal of employee empowerment. With that in mind, she has moved Brian along a series of small steps, or approximations, until the final result was achieved. In your own organisation there may be any number of successive approximations needed to achieve your own goals, some of which you may choose to run simultaneously.

The advantage you have with the successive approximation approach is that the focus is usually on each one of the steps, rather than on the final outcome. While beginning with the end in mind is important, you do need to look where you are going or you might step into an open manhole!

DO UNTO OTHERS

One of the key factors in attracting and retaining staff is the role of inspirational managers. Identify people who have this potential. Look at the relationships they develop. Do others readily turn to them for advice? Are they good listeners? When recruiting people to your cause, paint an honest picture of what managing people will be like and what you want to achieve. If possible, first make use of informal support like mentoring or coaching rather than line management responsibilities. Initially, you may not even be able to give your potential inspirational managers line management responsibilities.

You need to be an inspirational manager, mentor or coach to help your allies to see the benefits that this type of management can bring. Remember that inspirational managers and average managers can have the same formal responsibilities – it's the passion and commitment in delivery that makes people inspirational. Your job is to help them find that passion.

Of course, you also need to make sure that there is some form of reward and recognition for displaying the appropriate behaviour. Even if rewards are not formal, don't forget to feed their energy. At the very least, staff and managers will need praise, support and encouragement as well as help in evaluating how your now-shared project is moving forward. Don't overlook the importance of training and development as a motivational tool. Regular and constant up-skilling can be a powerful motivational alternative in an environment that is not directly focused on reward and recognition. All of the types of bosses we outlined in Chapter 2 can be inspirational. In this context we're talking more about managers than bosses, but the same traits can apply. No one style is better than another: it's the appropriate application of a particular style in the correct context that yields these inspirational results.

TEACH A MAN TO FISH

The following quotation serves as a useful overview: *"I hear – I forget; I see – I remember; I do – I understand."* To which we can add, *"I teach – I commit"*. In other words, if someone is simply told something or listens passively to a lecture, there is little chance that they'll remember all they're told.

Watching someone in action is, for most people, a far more effective way of learning. Actually doing the task is even better. How many of us have watched someone doing something that looks very easy, only to find it's much more difficult than we thought? But, by practising, we get better and better and understand more about the task. Finally, by teaching others, we're forced to respond to their queries and failures and become masters of the task. At each level (listening, watching, doing, teaching), your degree of involvement becomes greater. That's powerfully motivating.

If this coaching and mentoring takes place, then:

- Staff will feel more valued
- It will legitimise the training they receive (which in turn will add to their perception of your organisation as the preferred employer)
- You will gradually be developing an organisational culture that motivates people and supports them in their development.

This buzz will translate into better service and will be picked up by clients and that, in turn, translates into a more profitable business. Happy, motivated staff impact positively on the customer experience, and that impacts positively on your business.

While the present culture is shaped in the boss' image, you need people to understand that even though he may not change, the way things get done in an organisation *can* change. We all know of organisations where things get done despite the systems rather than because of them. Your job in coaching people (including your boss) is, wherever possible, to help them see how things can be better and to help them discover what they can do to help this process and to take ownership of it. Look for informal, unplanned and unscheduled opportunities to coach and develop people. Waiting for a formal coaching session will result in many opportunities being missed. Just think of all the examples of how you've learnt things without expecting to, simply by working with colleagues, hearing a snatch of conversation or doing something for the first time because the usual person wasn't there and someone had to do it!

You should encourage the staff to be responsible for their actions and their results and to use their initiative and ingenuity. The goal is to create a partnership where staff give their total commitment to a cause that has become their own.

WALK TOWARDS THE LIGHT

Situational Leadership II *(Blanchard)* is a simple model designed to help move people towards high levels of commitment and competence. Whilst the principles are relatively simple to explain in a few lines, the practical application and nuances make attending a Situational Leadership II course a very worthwhile investment in your personal development – especially if you truly want to lead by example. Essentially, the model works on modifying the levels of support and direction you give someone based on *their* levels of competence and commitment.

The ability to accurately identify your associate's levels of commitment and competence is a key starting point in the successful application of this model. You need to have a willingness and ability to look at the situation and contextually assess the developmental needs of associates in order to decide which leadership style is most appropriate for the goal or task at hand. It is *stopping to think before you act*. This requires well-developed communication skills – most importantly *listening*

You must ensure that sufficient time is spent with each associate for trust and understanding to develop. This is essential if you wish to prevent misunderstandings, maintain and grow your relationship and ensure their co-operation and participation.

By improving your skills in this area you will find you not only gain a greater sense of job satisfaction but also benefit from significant time-saving. This time-saving applies both to knowing where and how best to direct your own efforts and to the gains the organisation will make because of your input. And you can do this without necessarily having improved your own task-specific time management or organisational skills! By sorting out the problems in the copy department, Brian has freed himself up time-wise without improving his time management or organisational skills.

TELLING IS NOT ENOUGH

Intuition may lead us to believe that information transfer

is enough to ensure a behavioural modification. How often do we hear colleagues complaining about staff who, despite having been told a thousand times, still do not follow advice? The innately good communicators seem to have less of a problem. Those who do not have this skill become more and more frustrated and attempt to effect change by applying some sort of information overload or by adopting one of the poor leadership models described above (adversarial, patriarchal or silent). Only those with well-developed self-awareness are able to be inclusive and entrepreneurial.

Generally, simply giving someone information is not sufficient to change their behaviour. For example, simply knowing that smoking is bad for you is generally insufficient to get people to stop smoking. Meaningful change requires more. Society's attitude to smoking needs to change (it's now really only baddies who smoke on television or in the movies). In addition, changes of behaviour have been introduced to prevent smoking in vehicles, the workplace or pubs as well as prohibiting minors from buying cigarettes. This supports studies which have shown that people will respond positively to most messages provided these address three needs or aspects more-or-less simultaneously – **knowledge, attitude** and **behaviour**. The message should impart information, engender the correct attitude or desire and ultimately result in a change in or reinforcement of the desired behaviour.

Feelings must also be influenced and systems need to be set in place to ensure that staff act appropriately and are rewarded for doing so. Mutual trust is required in order to ensure that staff are open and receptive to your messages. In essence, you need to present yourself not only as competent but, depending on the circumstance, also caring, sympathetic and understanding. Jo's managed to move hearts and minds, as well as provide leadership and direction, by making people feel heard and understood and by giving direction (or nudges!) at the appropriate time.

DO UNTO OTHERS. AGAIN

There are ways in which any manager can be inspirational. By leading by example, for instance. Inspiring behaviour can be more powerful than inspiring speech. Going out and speaking to the complaining client personally while others watch will inspire them to do the same. Have big ideas (a vision) and be open to the big ideas of others. Listening to their ideas and building them into yours will inspire them to give you more ideas. Try to encourage innovation and then provide focus while encouraging communication, dialogue and feedback. Asking for new ways of working can inspire your team to think of these ideas, and to encourage others to do so in turn.

To inspire, you should plan for progress. You need to be focused and to have the ability to remain so, while working on building momentum. Try to be known for putting people first and treating them as individuals. Give praise! Be approachable, honest and consistent. Empower your team, remove obstacles to their performance and trust them to deliver. At all times, focus on your role and not your profile.

As far as possible, you need to create an environment that motivates people. We agree with the Good to Great team in suggesting the following steps:

- Questioning – in order to gain insight into situations or issues. Ask the questions that will lead to the team sharing their insights. Simply asking someone how they would solve a problem, and then listening to their solution, would be a suitable start.
- Dialogue and debate – involve people in uncovering the solutions to their problems. Encourage the team to question you and not to take things at face value. The more debate there is (well, within reason!) the more robust the end ideas will be and the better they're likely to work in practice.
- Don't blame – focus rather on learning and understanding to prevent future recurrences. Inviting the team to audit its own results can work extremely well. Simply sitting down together to look at what went right, what worked less well and what needs to change can be very motivating.
- Encourage your team – to develop early warning systems for system or process failures, and to pay heed to those signs. A red flag system that stops a process and forces a review is a powerful tool for change.

Look for opportunities to ensure that your team applies as many of the above principles as possible. Try to influence those you work with to adopt these principles.

WALK THE TALK

For true credibility, you must 'live' your cause and embrace the values that will support the process. If Ghandi hadn't been willing to go on a hunger strike to the point of death, if needed, for what he believed in, he would not have achieved the support or the success that he did. Some people may hope for you to fail and could use this to damage your credibility, adversely affecting your ability to influence others or make changes to the organisation. We therefore recommend that you commit to embracing and wholeheartedly applying the following points, based on suggestions by Stephen Covey:

- Being proactive
- Being open to new ideas
- Being willing to take calculated risks
- Looking for learning in the challenges with which you are presented
- Being self-critical
- Viewing disagreement as a sign of interest and engagement.

Beware of overestimating your abilities, including your ability to endure adversity for prolonged periods. If at all possible, we recommend that you invest in a coaching or mentoring relationship with someone who has the ability to understand the situation in which you find yourself. Having a good coach or mentor can help you to prioritise, as well as reinforcing lessons and helping you to better apply them. You need to be a source of inspiration and motivation to others, but who is going to look after you? At the end of the previous chapter, Jerry was concerned about Jo and her ability to take on the challenge. His concern there was mostly about her stamina, but her ability to gain the new skills and retain the objective perspective she'll need will depend, to a large degree, on the quality of the support she receives.

Others can often be better at assessing our stamina and levels of competence than we are. This might be an area where you should regularly get an external appraisal in order to gain a more objective perspective of how well you are likely to deal with a given situation.

In this chapter, we have stressed the importance of processes rather than solutions. We also recommend that you consider which critical success factors were required to move the organisation in the appropriate direction. Any change takes time and, while you may have an idea of your ideal timetable, you need to be flexible about this.

IT'S NOT A RACE

In Collins' study it took companies up to four years to achieve clarity of purpose within their business.

Depending on the size and the scope of the project you are undertaking, you would be well advised to set your expectations of overall success in terms of years rather than months. Also, progress should be measured in terms of sequences of events rather than their timely occurrence. It's more important to reach milestones safely and in the right order than to cause harm by trying to stick to an artificial deadline. Prioritise the issues and decide on the sequence in which they should occur. This will help to give you a rough map against which you can log progress.

Your plan will almost certainly require regular review and modification, but it's worth writing it down. The benefits of having a rough written plan are twofold:

1) Being able to see the distance travelled can be very motivating, especially when you suffer a setback, as will happen from time to time.

2) You have a running order against which to prepare yourself. As you pass one milestone, you have an idea of which tools, skills or resources are required to reach the next stage. This is important because not everything will be in an immediate state of readiness. You need to assess what critical success factors may be missing. A lack of business planning may be addressed relatively easily: it isn't difficult to understand what's required in a plan and to sit down and write one. But a lack of vision beyond the mere maintenance of the status quo will probably require less readily available business or strategic skills. You may need time to find

or develop the necessary resource so that it is ready to use when you or the organisation needs it. On occasion, you may even be working one or two steps ahead of what is currently required. Jo could have had a draft copy of a staff empowerment tool ready to use at the time that Brian was still yelling at Mel to stop bullying Sarah.

BE PREPARED

If at all possible, try to ensure that all critical requirements that help your cause are directly or indirectly sourced by you. We have seen many situations where alternative sources are utilised, bringing unforeseen influences that hamper your cause – or even work directly against it. In our bullying example, it could be a mistake for Jo to let Brian go off and find someone to give him advice. That advice might be to get legal protection for the organisation that prevents lawsuits against Simian for bullying and harassment. This might make Brian happy, but would fail to deal with the real issue. If Jo can stay in control of the source of advice, it's far more likely that the real priority of developing staff empowerment will be met.

Whilst the introduction and adoption of new systems and processes or the abolition of old ones may be easy milestones by which you can gauge successes or failures, success can also be measured through changes in perception and attitudes. There are additional factors, like reduced staff turnover, that could be significant indicators of progress from your initiatives. You may not need to consult a sociologist or market researcher to ensure your observations are as objective as possible; you should have a pretty good idea of where things are going and the progress you are making. These experts are useful, however, in helping ensure that you do not draw erroneous conclusions from the data you collect.

Jo's friend, Kumar, is a statistics major. He tells a story that illustrates our point very nicely:

"Look at the incidence of motor vehicle accidents in cities and towns. You'll find that there's a strong positive correlation between the presence of zoos in the town and an increased number of car accidents. No sane person thinks it's the zoos causing the accident, so what's going on?

"This is because of what we very clever statisticians call a spurious variable. There is a third factor, the 'lurking' or 'confounding variable' that gives rise to each of the two factors we are examining. In the case of our example it's population size. The larger the population of a town, the higher the chance there will be more accidents and the greater the chance there will be a zoo.

"If you're unaware of this confounding variable, you are likely to draw the wrong conclusions from your findings. That could impact on how you intend to apply them to future problems. You could end up banning zoos!"

This book focuses on the changes you want to bring about and how you can best achieve them. Your agenda is to improve what already exists. If something good has to be sacrificed, you should ensure that you have supported or developed capabilities or performances that are even better. Our waterskiing analogy in Chapter 3 demonstrates how you sometimes need to sacrifice performance in the short-term for greater achievement in the longer term. Charlotte, our waterskier, had to abandon some of her performance in order to develop a new technique that, ultimately, allowed her to surpass her previous levels of achievement. This is far more critical in the early stages of the project, because significant setbacks at this stage could put an end to any or all of your initiatives or ideas for good!

It may seem odd that you are being encouraged to keep your agenda to yourself while we have earlier said, quite clearly, that hidden agendas are to be avoided in the boss or the organisation. The two are different, however. A hidden agenda in an organisation results in tension between the stated aim of the company and its actual goal. It might say it's all about quality of service while it's actually all about profit. This causes tension and loss of morale. Similarly, your boss' hidden agenda will be equally corrosive.

In your case, your agenda is hidden only from those who might react badly to it because of lack of understanding. It's perfectly clear to your followers and allies. And, little by little, it will become clear to everyone, including your boss. Just like our sales model, it's a matter of timing; had Jo just asked Brian for an empowerment policy it might never have happened. By using successive approximation and gauging Brian's levels of interest accurately, Jo was able to develop the process until the empowerment policy became inevitable.

If required to disclose any part of your agenda, consider the following:

- To whom are you disclosing it – friend or foe?
- What is their level of interest? How much detail do they need?
- Where in relation to the tipping-point are you? If you are still in the early stages of gaining allies, you could risk major setbacks by overplaying your hand, especially to the wrong person.
- Why is this information required? No matter how well trusted a person is, there's much to be gained in first asking why they want the information. Besides being a useful stalling tactic, it also helps to ensure that you can meet their needs as well as possible.

Jerry's taken Jo out to dinner to celebrate four months with SimianSynergy. Jo is frustrated and annoyed because George, one of her greatest allies at work, has point blank refused to go along with a strategy she's proposed. She can't understand why he is resisting staff empowerment.

"I can't understand what went wrong! I know George likes and trusts me. And I'm pretty sure we share the same vision. Why won't he come on board?"

"Well…" says Jerry. "From what you say, I'd put

George in the committed but not yet convinced category. Is that about right?"

"Yes, I'd say so."

"So what approach do you think would work best?" asks Jerry.

"Hmm. I suppose I might have moved to the end of the process too quickly for him. I probably spooked him!" Jo chuckles. "I guess I need to work on selling my ideas a bit better!"

That's a good point, Jo. Whether you're persuading or selling, there are techniques that can help you to do this better. Let's have a look at some of these, and the principles involved, in the next chapter.

SELLING YOUR IDEAS
– THE BASICS

THE CRUNCHY BIT

Sales, for us, is about helping people to make informed buying decisions, rather than flogging them something that's of no benefit to them. In the context of attempting to change the organisation, you need to regard everyone you work with as a potential customer – both within and outside the business.

Our sales are not 'transactional' – they don't simply involve handing over goods or ideas in exchange for something. It's 'relationship' selling, based on the depth of understanding you have of your customer and your knowledge of what will benefit them. These sales are built on the bedrock of trust.

You need to understand what makes your customers tick: are they interested in their own opinions or received wisdom? Do they move towards pleasure or away from pain? Are they interested in the detail, or just the big picture? Knowing all this helps you to tailor your sale to their needs in the way that'll be most readily understood and accepted. There are other techniques that will help you: asking the right questions and listening actively, repeating what the customer has said, and providing options or alternative solutions. The end result is that the customer feels that you understand him and is much more willing to listen to your suggestions and advice.

We recommend applying the techniques of principle, not position. Present arguments to your customer based on their needs, rather than seeing it as some sort of competition between you and the customer, where someone wins and someone loses. Separating the people from the problem allows the issue to be dealt with on its own merits. This approach engenders trust and collaboration, and helps you to sell your ideas.

EVERYONE'S A CUSTOMER

This chapter is all about sales. Let's go back a bit and recap what we mean by 'selling'. The things we're selling here, as we explained in Chapter 7, are your ideas. It's a process of convincing other people that your ideas and philosophies are relevant and appropriate to your organisation. Bear in mind that everyone, from your boss down, is a potential 'customer'. In order to succeed with your vision for the organisation, you need allies. You need to create a groundswell for your ideas by recruiting people to your cause.

To expand a little on the role of your boss: he's a critical part of the process. While you may be forced to go ahead in spite of him, it is far better to have him alongside you as an ally. This book was written to help you to succeed in spite of your boss, but if there are even a few elements of your plan that he's willing to support, your task will be much easier.

In order to sell your vision, you need to keep the principles of 'relationship selling' very much in mind. In relationship selling, the focus is truly to help the customer make the correct buying decision, even where that means recognising that what you're selling isn't what the other person needs right now. Let's take another leaf from *The Forum Corporation*:

THEY'RE ALL INDIVIDUALS

1) Focus on each and every 'customer' involved:

- concentrate on their agendas and needs – not your own
- make sure everything you do is vital to the process of selling your vision, and that that is valuable to the 'customer'
- always try to remember the WIIFM question: 'What's in it for me?' Consider both long and short-term benefits to the customer.

Jerry gives Jo an example: "Do you remember when we put the deposit down on our flat?" he asks. "The salesman was very clever. He asked over and over again what we wanted in a flat. He made sure he knew exactly what we were looking for – a couple of spare rooms – and then showed us what he had that was closest to what we wanted. The reason we wanted the extra rooms was to have somewhere to have your folks over when they were in town. The first agent found us a flat that had two spare rooms, which was perfect, but neither one was *en suite*, which was a problem. The next agent listened to what we needed, not what we said we wanted, and found us our current flat. It had only one spare room, but was en suite – and suited our priorities better. It wasn't perfect, but it gave us the one thing we really wanted."

Exactly so: by focusing on what your potential allies really want to change, you can tailor your 'pitch' to each one.

YOU CAN TRUST ME. REALLY, YOU CAN

2) Earn their trust in you:

- remember that mild interest is not sufficient for you to pitch the full product (don't try to 'close the sale')
- address concerns at each step before progressing to the next one
- always try to be a problem solver.

As we saw in the example above, the first agent heard Jerry and Jo ask for two spare bedrooms and showed them what he thought they wanted. The next agent, on the other hand, listened to what they actually needed and showed them a flat that gave them that.

TEACH A MAN TO FISH

3) Persuade through involvement. As we saw in Chapter 7, a good coach increases levels of involvement by moving

his pupils from simply hearing something to seeing it done, then to doing it themselves and, finally, to teaching the task:

- people tend to believe more what they say themselves rather than what others say to them, so let the customer speak
- getting information from people and giving them a choice of responses is at least as important as providing information
- talk less and listen more: whilst general listening is great and shouldn't be overlooked, at some stage in the 'buying' cycle you will need to ask the right questions. The answers to these are especially critical in terms of 'selling' your idea. Try to ask questions which encourage the customer to think, evaluate, analyse or express feelings. These questions not only increase involvement but are like drilling for oil: it's there, but if you don't drill deep enough, you might not find anything
- try always to see opposition as a sign of involvement, especially with those in the 'useful ally' camp
- involve people in determining their needs and exploring options for solutions. It's better to give them the skills to identify or discover a solution for themselves than to give them the answer on a platter.

What the second agent did was to ensure that he really understood his clients. He looked at Jo and Jerry and asked why they needed the extra rooms. They told him about

Jo's parents, and the agent then asked how old they were and what they would need in the flat to make them comfortable. The agent told them about his own parents, who were a similar age, which allowed him to empathise with Jo and Jerry and for them to feel that he really did understand them. Finally, once he was sure he understood their needs correctly, he showed them a smaller flat than the first one but one that gave them the setup they needed. And that saved them a little money, too!

Underpinning this process will be the need to build a personal bond or rapport through the ability to empathise, as well as other mirroring techniques. Didn't the agent do that well by talking about his own parents?

FEATURES AND BENEFITS

By now you will have identified current and potential strategic supporters within and outside the organisation. When talking to your chosen potential supporters, you will find that if you have asked the right questions, you should more easily be able to talk to them in terms of benefits – making the process real and increasingly desirable for them. The features of the flat the agent showed Jo and Jerry were two bedrooms and two bathrooms. The benefits, on the other hand, were that the second bedroom was *en suite*, offering Jo's parents greater convenience and comfort by avoiding the need for them to leave their room for a comfort break in the middle of the night.

Also remember to exude enthusiasm for the changes

you desire, or you are likely just to be seen as a whiner and to alienate yourself.

The overriding perspective with your supporters should be to move them away from an initial lack of interest in your offer. As you move them gradually to levels of increasing interest and desire to obtain your vision of the alternative future, their own level of enthusiasm will increase and they will become drivers, working for change alongside you.

At each step of the way you will have to retain the approach we've outlined, but the process may require modification depending on the supporter's level of interest.

I BELIEVE IN ME. NO, ACTUALLY, I BELIEVE IN YOU

Another useful consideration is whether or not the person you are trying to influence deals primarily with an internal or an external frame of reference. In simple terms this means that some people look for evidence to support an argument from external sources e.g. statistics, reports or other people. Others tend to just 'know' whether they like something or not. If you can identify this and use it to your advantage it could prove a very useful lever in moving things in the desired direction. As previously discussed, by focusing on the client, and really listening to what they say and how they say it, you can develop an insight into their frame of reference.

FOREST OR TREES?

To develop the theme further, we can also divide people into two groups based on whether or not they are big picture or detail people. Again, when presenting arguments to a big picture person you need to focus on the whole as a unit or you run the risk of boring them. Conversely, the detail people will in no way be swayed with any argument that does not address the nitty-gritty of the issues that concern them. Most people, however, are not at these extremes but along a continuum. As we keep saying, knowing your client is of paramount importance. In this case, knowing the right amount of detail to give will be a result of knowing him or her really well.

We have given you a brief overview of the selling process for your ideas. We previously identified that you will, in all likelihood, be dealing with more than one potential supporter. It is, therefore, necessary also to consider the general principles applied to managing complex customers or accounts. The challenge is to recognise the different needs and skill sets of the various people involved in the decision-making process. For example, technical people may be more concerned with performance and specific problems while the financial experts are focused on the bottom line. The key is to gain trust in this complex environment by being able to adapt to the varying styles of those you seek to influence – by mirroring them, for example.

Jo comes up with her own example for Jerry. "I guess

that's like when you bought your new car," she says. "The salesman saw at once you were a petrol head and got you talking in huge detail about torque ratios, flanges and ganglepins. When he spoke to me, though, he focused on the fuel economy and how 'green' the car was. Very clever of him!"

Jo's salesman recognised, too, that decisions are often made by more than one person. Or, in your case, there may be a number of people who influence the decisions made by your boss.

You need to understand the dynamics of power within the organisation clearly. You need to know both the explicit and implicit ethos of the group. And you need to understand the varying drives and values of the individual players within the group. This is not nearly as daunting as it sounds – there's no need to go on a major fact-finding or spying expedition. You are reading this book because you have had time to recognise that you are frustrated in your ambitions for the organisation. You will by now also know who your supporters are, what their drives, ambitions and fears are, and have a good idea of how your company works and its unspoken values. Moving forward from here you need the guidance that this book offers.

AGONY AND ECSTACY

Most motivational coaches agree that the principles of pleasure and pain feature strongly in moving us in a particular direction. We tend to move away from pain or a negative stimulus and toward pleasure or a positive stimulus. This is self-evident, but can be used in moving your supporters toward your ideas by demonstrating the 'pain' caused by the *status quo* and the relative pleasure that adopting your ideas will bring. In Jo's own career path, she left her previous job to get away from the frustration she was having with lack of recognition, low pay and limited opportunities for progression. She moved to SimianSynergy because, as we saw in Chapter 1, Brian was a legendary figure in the industry, offered a better salary and she anticipated rapid advancement within Simian. She moved, in other words, away from 'pain' and towards 'pleasure'.

Similarly, it might be used the same way on the boss, but he is much less likely to see any pain associated with his way of doing things – it's just that other people don't have his immaculate 20:20 vision!

Some experts will argue that some people tend to be primarily driven away from things whilst others are driven towards things. Another school of thought says that the initial driver is a move away from discomfort, and the incentive for continuing along that path is the move towards a positive outcome.

Your inner belief that your organisation can be great may not be enough to sustain you. You will already have a clear vision of your organisation's end point and have drawn positive feedback from any small steps in that direction. Identify the factors that are pivotal in achieving your milestones. Unlike traditional strategic planning, you shouldn't hold your organisation to too rigid a time schedule unless failure to meet your deadlines will prompt your exit.

A MATTER OF PRINCIPLE

In moving forward, it would be beneficial to take advantage of the processes involved in principled negotiation rather than the classical approach of positional negotiation.

In principled negotiation, you focus on the problem, not on interpersonal issues or animosities. Look for common interests – which may simply be avoiding disaster! – create options to work from and clarify how to evaluate these options objectively. Finally, know your limits: what is the point at which you'd do better to walk away?

Positional negotiation is the old-style, win/lose trade off of the zero-sum game. It tends to be linked to ego and driven by dominance. The classic 'if you do this for me, I'll do that for you' is an example of positional negotiation.

Remember that even though negotiation on the final position may not be on your agenda, the entire process is a negotiation towards a sale: the sale of your ideas. You want to help people to buy – first your supporters and, finally, the boss.

THERE'S NO NEED TO GET PERSONAL

It's important not to get personal about the problem i.e. you may not like the boss but you need some level of objectivity in order to deal with obstacles – letting personal issues cloud your judgement will hamper progress. Focus on interests rather than positions. One of the most famous examples of this is found in *Getting to Yes*, the classic 1981 title. Fisher and Ury tell the story of the two sisters fighting over an orange. The sisters love each other and agree to split the orange in half. The first sister eats her half of the fruit and throws away the peel. The other uses the peel for baking and throws away the fruit. How much better off would they have been if they'd focused on interests rather than positions, understood each other's needs and looked at common solutions?

Before you do anything or encourage others to act, generate and explore options and create scenarios: think of the consequences of potential courses of action – and inaction. For everything you do or choose not to do, there will be results. You need to judge which of the possible actions and outcomes will serve your purposes best.

By applying these simple principles, you'll be surprised at how much closer you will be moving towards the sales philosophy and away from positional negotiation. Where possible, base any agreements on objective criteria or fair procedures. Finally, before you totally commit to the process, make sure that you have considered what the alternatives are should you decide to walk away. Fisher and Ury's phrase for this is 'BATNA' – your Best Alternative to a Negotiated Agreement.

Your efforts are unlikely to yield an appreciative or positive response every time. In fact, you are more likely to receive a hostile and emotional reaction to any perceived loss of control by the boss and other senior managers. When this happens, you will need to excel at listening, validating his viewpoint and empathising. Always be mindful of the 'big picture' and don't let ego tempt you to win a battle at the expense of the war.

This is an area that requires a lot of work, but the key to success lies in:

- Beginning with the end in mind (you must have a very clear idea of where you want to end up)
- Always being prepared
- Being proactive (if you are very clear of what you need to do, there will be opportunities for you to get your foot in the door. Always try to make every situation an opportunity to apply the successive approximation technique we explained in Chapter 6)
- Perfect timing (opportunities will present themselves and if you are not ready to place the right Jenga® piece in the right place, you may have to wait a long time for that opportunity to come around again)
- Building support for your cause. (The more people who collaborate with you, the more likely you will be able to induce strategic change through popular support. As the diagram, on the next page, shows, popular support can move the organisation forward before its formal strategy, structures and policies have changed.)

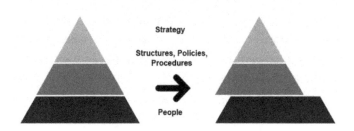

Strategy

Structures, Policies, Procedures

People

THE CUSTOMER IS ALWAYS RIGHT

Look for the chance to introduce some form of customer service mentality within the group. This is a unified approach within an organisation to outstanding customer experience. Aim to constantly and consistently exceed the customer's expectations. This may relate to external customers only, but is readily extended to internal 'customers', too. Everyone, at all levels of the organisation, is treated well.

Whether this is formal or informal is not important. If you can get formal endorsement for it this will go a long way towards freeing up resources and developing some form of infrastructure to work with.

A critical component of this new customer service training initiative is the introduction of the *internal customer* concept. The customer service initiative gives you the opportunity to incorporate respect and relationships into the process of organisational transformation. This is critical because respect, recognition and relationships are considered by many to be the ultimate source of competitive advantage. Give employees a voice and, instead of talking about performance, they refer to the positive motivational effects of managers who respect them and recognise their contributions, as well as the effects of friendships at work. Soldiers die for their comrades; sportsmen risk career-threatening injury for their team. Your staff will be happy to give extra effort if they feel motivated, appreciated and important.

By using this approach you will be able to work, albeit indirectly, on the development of good management and firming up the foundations of the company.

The customer service angle also gives you an indirect way to address inadequate cooperation within the organisation. It can help to motivate, engage with and empower people in the face of an obstructive or restrictive system. This is vital to moving people in the organisation in the direction both you and they want to go.

We think it worthwhile to highlight the importance of 'selling' your idea to the boss. Even if you consider yourself a good salesperson, you would be wise to revisit the strategies and approaches through which you present ideas to him. Despite above-average competencies in certain areas, we often tend to overlook certain basic steps, or sometimes rush the process and find ourselves unable to 'close' effectively. Before moving on, it is essential to make sure that you have at least tried to 'sell' one or two ideas to the boss by following the relationship sales process through very carefully. You may have more success than you anticipate! And, as stated near the start of this chapter, he may be amenable to at least some of your suggestions.

In all your interactions, remember the three guiding principles:

- focus on his agenda and issues, not yours
- gain his trust and gain access to more confidential, personal information
- encourage as much involvement as possible and use this process as a persuasive tool.

To maximise impact you need to excel at the following communication tools:

CONTACT? CONTACT!

1) Connecting: How well can you establish a personal bond with your boss?
This personal bond is what is needed to establish a long-term relationship. Often this happens naturally because of some form of 'chemistry' between people. If this chemistry is absent, you have to work harder to establish a bond. Be natural. Sincerity is vital!

Tips to connect effectively:

- Establish and maintain eye contact
- Adapt by using similar phrases, speech patterns,

gestures and body postures (at the very least, they must be *compatible* with those of your boss)

- Smile, use small-talk, establish areas of common interest, use a genuine compliment if possible

It's important not to come over as false or condescending, especially if the chemistry is absent between you and your boss. Make sure to be genuine in your intention to understand his needs and drives rather than concentrating on any one sales technique.

ARE YOU LISTENING TO ME?

2) Listening: This must be active and can be divided into two areas:

A) ***Reinforcing*** *and empathising* – involving the boss in the discussion

- How to keep him involved
- Use supportive words and phrases to indicate you want to hear more. Make sure your non-verbal communication does not contradict this! Don't yawn and say, "That's really interesting."
- Empathising does **not** imply you agree with him – merely that you *understand* e.g. "That must be very frustrating."
- Show that you have *heard and understood* the information. (See Confirming)

B) *Questioning* – helps you get in-depth information about the situation and the boss's real needs. Tips to improve the way you formulate your questions:

- Ask 'open' questions i.e. these questions cannot be answered by a 'yes' or a 'no', for example use questions that begin with "what", 'why' or 'how'.
- Ask questions that require your boss to think, evaluate, analyse, speculate or express feelings when he gives you an answer.

IF I'VE HEARD YOU RIGHT...

3) Confirming: This helps you make sure that you have understood him properly.

- Regularly restate or paraphrase what he has said, even if you are 100% certain you know what it is. Make sure that what *you* think is important is what the *he* thinks is important e.g. "Does that accurately summarize what you explained to me?" Let him be certain that you understand – that will give him a feeling of security and elevate you to someone who 'gets it'.
- Make sure that you check that the boss is also in agreement with everything you have said so far.

SO, WHAT'S TO BE DONE?

4) Providing: This helps you to create a clear, positive image of your competencies and what you can offer.

- Speak primarily of the benefits i.e. what your suggestions will do or achieve is not important. Rather, explain how they will satisfy his needs.
- Speak briefly and keep to the point.
- Be enthusiastic: enthusiasm is one of the most contagious positive emotions.

Finally, don't forget to assess his levels of interest and apply the appropriate approach in order to move him forward (see Chapter 2 for further detail on this). Do make sure that you don't come over as patronising! The principles are effective, however, whether dealing with a subordinate or with your boss.

Earlier, we saw Brian dealing with Mel's bullying of Sarah. Brian said, *"I've told Mel to stop picking on Sarah, but it's because she's such a flower. She's asking for it! Now I need to go and speak to Mel again when it's really Sarah who should be told off. What a pain!"*

Brian's level of interest was low, as we said in that chapter, but he was clearly frustrated. If Jo wants Brian to feel heard and understood, she'd do well to reinforce his feelings and empathise with him. Something along the lines of, "This must be so frustrating! It's so annoying when people won't behave!" She could ask, "How many times has this happened? Is this a frequent problem with them?" That would demonstrate further interest on her part and encourage Brian to tell her more about it.

IF YOU CAN'T GO THROUGH, GO AROUND

If you have followed all these steps carefully and closely on a few occasions and are still unable to see any improvement, you may be justified in moving towards working on achieving change or progress despite, rather than through, your boss. Even if you do progress down this route, it is essential to remember always to look for opportunities to plant seeds with the boss, to try to move him forward even if only by small steps. Remember, every little move in the right direction will help increase the momentum. The closer he is towards your end goal, the less likely it is that he will see it as being diametrically opposed to his thinking. In fact, the changing landscape you create can often result in him changing his perspective all by himself.

The introduction of a process designed to encourage respect and relationships is likely to be welcomed by the boss especially since this is most likely what he wants the staff to show customers. Timing is important. You will probably not have to wait long for a crisis caused by poor customer service to occur.

Now is the time to apply your sales techniques and help the boss identify the gap between where the organisation presently is and where he would like it to be in terms of customer service. Even if he has done this himself, your job is to create an enhanced need, a desire to want to move towards the attainment of higher levels of customer service since this will invariably give him what he is looking for: commercial success. Through the use of a few well planned and phrased questions, you should help increase his desire to want to move away from the current problem and towards the better future.

Ensure that you *don't* provide the solution. Help him explore options and examine the consequences of possible resolution. If he doesn't come up with a solution you may have to prompt him a little. Remember that if he comes up with this idea *by himself* he's less likely to oppose it and will give it stronger support. Whatever the route you take, you will arrive at an agreement that things need to be done to improve customer service, with you helping to drive or steer this initiative to a greater or lesser degree.

AND THE WINNER IS:

At this stage you will have achieved a significant step towards victory! You only need a few minor tweaks to this customer service programme in order to use it to spearhead much of your campaign to induce change through popular support.

We have highlighted the overriding principles you need to adopt in order to be able to succeed at relationship selling. Whether this is with your boss, a Powerful Other or a potential ally, you need to disregard your agenda and try to understand exactly where your customer's priorities lie. The old saying, *"I don't care how much you know until I know how much you care,"* aptly sums this up.

Understanding really only begins when you, figuratively, walk in the other person's shoes and try to experience their feelings. This does not mean you have to agree with their perspective but simply to understand how they think and feel. As most good sales people know, once you have done this well, the client is usually more likely to make the reciprocal effort to understand you. When you are truly interested in the points of view of others, that openness usually creates a climate that allows them to look at ideas, both theirs and yours, without feeling threatened. Most people find an inflexible assault distressing. If your boss is tell-assertive, this distress is likely to manifest itself as a *fight* response from him, which is unlikely to result in a positive outcome. Always try to avoid a frontal assault if possible. Keep your powder dry and keep your eye on the end result, not the immediate battle.

Body language, facial expressions and tone of voice are all important when actively listening. Your focus must be as absolute as possible. Many people are actually not very good at expressing their feelings but, if you understand how they feel, it goes a long way to developing the relationship and building trust. You will need trust if you want to move things on to the next stage. On an emotional level, people also feel safer when they sense we are trying to understand their feelings.

LET ME SEE IF I'VE UNDERSTOOD YOU CORRECTLY

Don't forget that the person you're talking to needs to know that you have heard and understood what he has told you. This is best done by paraphrasing and summarising what he has said, and only then moving on. If you do this properly, you should be able to express the 'client's' viewpoint even more accurately than he did.

For example, a home buyer might tell the agent a long story about their parents coming to visit and how good it is to have them over to stay, how they love going for walks in the park, that their favourite Italian restaurant has recently closed and that they suffer from embarrassing incontinence. The attentive estate agent or realtor will spot that what they need is a spare room with an *en suite* bathroom. He would then paraphrase by addressing their needs: the *en suite* prevents the parents from having to cross a landing at night and gives them convenience, privacy and security.

Listening and understanding is important not only in helping you to move towards 'closing' your sale, your agenda. It is also an essential principle to adopt if you wish to lead by example. You need the team to see that there is an efficient alternative to getting results. Through the regular application of this process, people should see some of the following benefits:

- The creation of opportunities through open exchange to facilitate and improve the process of problem solving

- Less fear
- The development of partnerships
- Increased trust and respect in relationships
- Higher levels of creativity and more honest dialogue.

Finally, the best thing about adopting this customer focus is that you can't lose! Even if you don't get a more co-operative attitude after the application of these techniques, you will definitely have more information than before – which can only help you.

> "That's all very well, Jerry, but what do I do when Brian's in one of his moods?"

That's a good question, Jo. The principles are the same irrespective of whether people are in good moods or when they're upset. It's the emphasis that changes. There are some additional skills that might be useful, though. Let's have a look at them in Chapter 9, starting with one of Brian's notorious tantrums.

SELLING YOUR IDEAS – ADVANCED TIPS AND TRICKS

THE CRUNCHY BIT

We've all been there: we've come up with a great idea and gone off to tell someone about it. But, instead of giving a positive response, the person you tell explodes! That's very disheartening. Don't be put off: rejection is a sign of engagement. You've clearly touched a nerve, so how can you work round their opposition? Redirecting this negative response in a positive direction is your challenge, and your opportunity to work with this 'difficult customer'.

We've all heard of 'fight or flight' reflexes. In our context, when faced with the 'fight' response, you'll need to be assertive (not aggressive), as well as applying the sales techniques we outlined earlier. In addition, you'll need to focus on solutions to their concerns. The 'run away' people need to feel heard, understood and protected, and to be given permission to express their concerns.

Sales is a constant, ongoing process. If everyone is a customer, it follows that everyone is a customer all the time! You'll need to keep up the successive approximation, listening, empathising, validating and summarising with everyone, always. This ongoing discussion focuses on benefits to the people involved. You'll be a coach and mentor in this process, too!

A sales pitch is all very well, but every good salesperson knows that you have to ask for the sale i.e. get some commitment to 'buy' from the customer. In our world, that means gaining a commitment to a change in behaviour, no matter how small.

Sad as it may seem, there is a good chance that, if you do your job subtly and well, the people you've empowered may not even recognise that it was you who helped them. You'll have to be prepared to get your kudos from the results you see, and not necessarily from the thanks you receive.

WHO'S THE DIFFICULT CUSTOMER?

It's a bad day at SimianSynergy. Brian's having a temper tantrum because Jo hasn't followed his advice to the letter. He's upset that, even though the outcome was perfect for the company, he fears that things might have gone wrong. He's afraid that Jo might have set a precedent, and is renowned for his view that the road to hell is paved with good intentions.

> "I can't believe this!" yells Brian. "I specifically took the time to tell you exactly what to do and you completely ignored me!"

It's possible that, in spite of your careful planning and the boss's perceived agreement, he'll regularly find a reason to disagree with what you're doing. But it's not a fatal problem:

he's already agreed that something must be done, so it's just a case of clarifying what. Treat an attack on you as an attack on the problem. He's engaged, so take advantage and help him to find an alternative method to get what he wants – remind him that he wants better client service!

If you are doing something that creates conflict or is perceived to undermine the boss's position, then aim to apply the standard principles you would use when dealing with customer complaints: don't argue. Apologise and empathise with the frustration, then agree to look into it and follow up. Bear in mind that the boss is also a customer and you are eventually going to have to get him on board, so dealing with an outburst is very much the same as dealing with a dissatisfied customer.

Your challenge is to see this conflict as being positive! Most people hate conflict and try to avoid it; only a small minority seem to love it and positively seek it out. If you do hate it, here are some pointers to help you to contextualise it and so deal with it better:

Remember that conflict:

- Helps open up discussion
- If handled properly, can help to get problems solved
- Increases engagement and levels of interest. The more people are involved with something, the greater the likelihood that they will be committed to something that comes out of it, especially if it is a positive outcome
- Helps release stored up emotions
- Can help develop strong and effective relationships.

Part of the problem you are experiencing is likely due to your boss being 'tell assertive' i.e. he uses a direct approach when attempting to influence or control the actions of others. If this were not the case, you would most probably not be reading this book.

FIGHT OR FLIGHT?

When stressed or faced with any form of significant opposition, such people tend to demonstrate a 'fight' reaction i.e. they become increasingly tell assertive, using strong words and resolute actions to blow off steam and discharge their tension. Their behaviour becomes confrontational and can be loosely divided into either autocratic or attacking behaviour.

Autocratic behaviour tends to be more results-focused and looks for reasons. Here people become forceful and demanding, trying to use facts, logic and reason to gain influence and control. The Results Rupert-type of boss (Chapter 2) usually decides on a course of action with compliance as the only available option. They do not listen to others' feelings and simply want an outcome – theirs. Autocratic behaviour uses fear to subordinate others with an insistence on compliance and obedience. Be aware that such people can see emotion as a sign of weakness!

Attacking behaviour manifests as the verbalisation of judgemental feelings with blaming and emotion frequently evident. Control here tends to be effected through the use of emotion and feeling. Attackers act as though they must prove they can win and consequently display aggression or hostility with little regard for the consequences.

When dealing with an emotional response to your actions by someone who is behaving like this, we suggest you apply the sales skills and techniques you have practised and honed using the approach outlined in Chapter 2.

There is a lot of overlap between the techniques used in sales outlined in Chapter 8 and the methods for dealing with opposition from your boss or anyone else. If anything, the skills need to be applied even more dextrously when dealing with an emotional pushback on your ideas. This is because it's just about impossible to counter emotion with reason. The emotional person needs to have their feelings recognised and addressed in order to bring them under control and allow a rational discussion to occur.

Listen
Listen attentively while he blows off steam, accepting what he says without judging. Use non-verbal behaviour to show that you are interested and concerned. Remain calm, relaxed and attentive. This is your secret weapon! If you blow your fuse, you lose.

Empathise
Share his concerns and empathise with him. He has reasons for being upset, so let him understand that you really understand him.

Seek Clarification

Once he has let off steam, try to get him to explain what caused his tension more precisely. The more he talks, the more you are likely to understand his make-up. This is useful not only now but also in the future. You need to get to a point where both of you fully understand what has caused the upset.

Formulate a Plan

Once you have clarified the cause, share your thoughts and ideas on the problem and, together, plan how to resolve it. Make sure that you don't get bullied into simply following his course of action. This is where being calm and applying Principled Negotiation is critical.

Commit to a course of Action

After identifying a possible solution, identify specific actions that each of you will commit to, unless there is a very valid reason to exclude him. Remember that if he actively helps in finding a solution that suits your cause, it becomes much more difficult for him to negate it at a later stage. Offer support and arrange a follow-up session at which you'll 'report back'. In reality, that gives you an opportunity to check on his progress and involvement! Notice how this fits perfectly with the concept in Chapter 8 of 'persuading through involvement'.

You cannot change anyone else's behaviour but you can

change yours – and others may then change theirs.

Your primary objective here is to avoid losing too much ground or having a path of action totally or permanently blocked.

To increase your effectiveness at resolving disputes or conflict, it is important to vary your style according to the particular situation.

An extra skill that will require working on but can help to increase your levels of assertiveness in these situations: is the careful use of language to help create a positive perception. It's not what you say, it's the way that you say it!

ASSERTIVE	WEAK
(creates a positive perception)	(creates a negative perception)
Let me find out for you	I don't know
I will do what I can to help	I do not think that I can do that
Here's what I can do to help	There's nothing I can do about your problem

Think about the words and phrases that are used by your team daily. What are they, and what kind of impression is created when people hear this language?

We've already showed you how to start driving a little wedge into the opportunity offered by a client service charter. You're doing a bit of ju-jitsu, using his desire for change via the charter to your own ends. There will almost certainly be a backlash of some sort, but if you don't oppose it and use it to find solutions the boss prefers, you maintain your forward momentum. Now you need to add a lever to open that crack a little wider.

EVERYONE'S A CUSTOMER – ALL THE TIME

The same techniques apply to recruiting people to your cause. We have outlined the method of increasing the likelihood of finding followers and have proposed that you categorise people according to their levels of interest and modify your approach in accordance with this. We will now look at how to harness the energy from the interest and enthusiasm you have created to help focus efforts on actually following your advice i.e. on practical actions.

Focus your efforts on:

- Moving people from simply being interested in following your advice to becoming convinced that your advice is the only appropriate solution to their problem – and then going out to convince others
- Effectively delivering recommendations to people in such a way that their enthusiasm remains high
- Encouraging people to make appropriate decisions.

With those who now have a strong interest in moving away from their present situation, your objective is to present them with solutions. Speak of benefits to them. As we discuss later in this chapter, knowing the difference between a *feature* and a *benefit* (see Chapter 8 for the example of how the estate agent relates the feature of the *en suite* bathroom to a benefit for Jo's parents i.e. their greater convenience) will help you get a favourable response from the client.

Once you have convinced them that it makes sense to take action and that the alternatives you have presented have value, you need to recommend a course of action and encourage them to make a decision regarding it. Summarise their needs and the positive consequences of action. Then link these to the benefits of what you are offering. This reminds them of the urgency to act and that your proposed solution is appropriate. Ask them to plan with you, contributing their own ideas to what you are suggesting as a way forward.

- Be concise: now is not the time to ramble – get to the point
- Be confident – act as if you expect them to take up your offer. Research has shown that if your voice, posture and choice of words communicate that you expect someone to agree, you are encouraging them to agree. If you show uncertainty at this point it could start to unravel what you have achieved so far
- Don't be afraid of silence – wait for an answer. By remaining silent, you are encouraging them to respond. Five seconds of silence can be a powerful tool at this stage
- Praise them for having decided to take action – it's a good decision! This is important for two reasons: it

helps reduce any doubts they may have with this choice and it allows you to communicate to them that your concern goes beyond just 'closing a deal' but rather in building a long-term collaborative relationship based on an earned trust.

Medical research has shown that better relationships between doctor and patient result in improved clinical outcomes, greater patient satisfaction and fewer malpractice complaints. By keeping the focus on the relationship rather than the technical, transactional nature of healthcare, patients respond better to treatments. The same holds true for your project to move your company forward: if the people you deal with feel that they have a relationship with you and have bought in to the process of change, they are more likely to take ownership of the project and to feel satisfied with the outcomes.

A PROPHET IN HIS OWN LAND

If you have successfully planted ideas, sold concepts and encouraged ownership of the cause, there is a good chance that people will not even remember many of the original ideas as yours. You may have to bite your tongue on those occasions when ideas, results and outcomes get enthusiastically discussed and people forget the role you played. Take heart from the fact that these victories help bring you all one step closer to getting to where you and your followers know the organisation has to go. The cause will gain far greater momentum by your helping to maintain momentum in a positive direction than by petty in-fighting over who should get the most kudos. Don't let your ego stand in the way of real progress. Humility does not always come easily. Remember, humble people don't think less of themselves, they just think less about themselves. If you need to find a silver lining, think about your own personal development and look at this as a form of helping to develop you into a great leader.

You would do well to remember that people tend to overestimate their own level of competence. In fact, we've seen Jo do just this!

Their enthusiasm for the cause can create unrealistic expectations of their levels of endurance, the likelihood of success of various projects, or the likely rate of change. As Jerry fretted at the end of Chapter 6, like most people, Jo has a tendency to start a project with all guns blazing and then to lose energy as the novelty wears off. The most famous example was her decision to take up fencing. She spent a fortune on all the expensive kit, instructional DVDs, signing up for private lessons and a year's membership at her local fencing club. Well, that lasted all of four lessons! You should find the subtle middle path of sustaining the highest levels of enthusiasm while tempering expectations. At all times, err on the side of caution. When looking at meeting staff expectations, it is far better to under-promise and over-deliver than to have to try to deal with the consequences of disillusionment and disappointment e.g. decreased levels of motivation or abandonment of the cause.

"That all makes sense, Jerry," Jo confirms. "But to maintain their enthusiasm, people need to be reminded what's in it for them."

"A-ha!" Jerry exclaims. "You're talking about 'benefits' rather than 'features'."

FEATURES AND BENEFITS, OR: THE 'SO WHAT?' QUESTION

Let's look at features and benefits. This is one of the most widely taught techniques in basic sales training. One can apply this consistently to all prospective clients whether they are external, internal or the boss. No matter how hard we try, we often tend to elaborate on the features and not arrive at a meaningful benefit to the client. Using the lead-up phrase, "which to you means that..." is a helpful way of trying to move from feature to benefit. If this hasn't been done well, you are likely to be confronted with a 'so what?' type of response. To minimise the likelihood of this happening, you need to have focused on the client at the start of the sale. Only by doing this will you have fully understood and identified what his 'hot buttons' are, what he regards as important. When you have found these hot button needs and express the features of your product in such a way that it becomes beneficial to the client, you should have no problem in progressing the sale.

"For example," Jerry goes on, "let's say you were selling the benefit of a 2-in-1 shampoo and conditioner.

Benefits would be that it's environmentally friendlier (only one container to dispose of). Or it might offer more convenience in terms of space (only one bottle in the shower rack) or in terms of use (wash and condition your hair in one step). Or it might offer better value (it may be cheaper than the price of a shampoo as well as a conditioner). These are all potential benefits."

That's a good point, Jerry. If you can identify your client's specific need, the impact of your proposed solution will be better. (Of course, in your case you'd read 'supporter' for 'client'.) And, if you are lucky, the client will provide you with other benefits – including some that you may not even have thought of! He might say that he's always in a rush in the mornings and a 2-in-1 approach will save him time. Some benefits might not have occurred to you because they are so specific to a particular client – but if he feels your interest in him as an individual he will join with you in stating benefits and actually help you to close your own sale!

To help kick-start you in this process, we have attempted to outline the organisational benefits of what you are trying to achieve (opportunities, reduced fear, partnerships, trust, creativity). Bear in mind, however, that true benefits are very specific to each person, so you will still need to add your "which to you means that…" to these.

Below are some suggested features of the changes you're trying to create, as well as how these may possibly give rise to benefits. Any individual benefit, as we've just seen, is specific to a particular stakeholder, so each of your supporters may perceive a different benefit from each of the features listed. And there's no guarantee that they will arise at all – this is just an example!

- Feature: Improved organisational capacity to identify problems proactively and prevent them
- Benefit:
    - Less crisis-management

- Feature: An increase in the number of opportunities to exercise control and provide coaching
- Benefits:
    - Improved productivity; and/or
    - A larger pool of future leadership talent; and/or
    - More people feeling 'ownership' of both the organisation and specific projects

- Feature: Improved productivity (the benefit, above, can be a feature, too!)
- Benefit:
    - Improved financial efficiency

- Feature: Greater solidarity and organisational support, especially in times of crisis
- Benefits:
    - Improved working relationships
    - Improved team spirit

- Feature: Greater levels of positive word-of-mouth

promotional activity to both internal and external customers

- Benefits:
  - Happier staff
  - Reduced stress
  - Lower absenteeism
  - Reduced staff turnover
  - Happier customers
  - Increased recruitment of people with the right attitude

- Feature: Decreased number of controls through improved compliance
- Benefits:
  - Better quality of work
  - Improved organisational efficiency
  - Improved compliance through improved commitment
  - A competitive edge that is not easily replicated

CLOSING THE DEAL

Earlier, we outlined the need to assess a client's or potential ally's level of interest and adjust your approach to match that. The aim is to build in others a passion and excitement in what you are proposing, and to gain their will to take action through ownership of the cause.

Never assume this commitment is there. Wait for a response indicating a personal decision to commit. Listen to how the response is stated ("I'd like to help" is not nearly as committed as "I'm going to do this today") and be sure to acknowledge it. Watch out for any side-stepping, resistance or diversions. If necessary, go back to a simplified plan e.g. get your ally to commit to taking a small first step: "Will you start contacting people today?" Make sure that you are supportive and help build his enthusiasm and excitement.

Be on the lookout for passive resistance or changing the subject. For example, if the reply to your question about contacting people today is to tell you about their new kitten (or any response that's not clearly affirmative) that would indicate resistance. It's then up to you to identify the source of resistance or excuses. These might include lack of time, reluctance to change work habits, fear of change or of repercussions, the system might not allow change (remember those monkeys?), or other people whose cooperation is required but not at all guaranteed.

Acknowledge the excuse and redirect attention to actions that the person can control. Be supportive and show empathy and understanding of the situation. If necessary, encourage the development of alternatives or contingency plans – every excuse or reason requires a response. If necessary, be prepared to take a step back – and then move two steps forward! Don't force the pace. If you move too fast or push too hard, your potential ally might not be able to cope or, worse, might see you as a bully – just another boss!

NUDGE, DON'T SHOVE

In addition to classical sales, much work has been done on how one can organise the context in which people make decisions. Richard Thaler and Cass Sunstein give many examples in their book, *Nudge*, on how this concept can and has made major improvements to people's lives. The underlying premise is that since we have so much to think about every day, we simply cannot think about and analyse everything. Therefore, we tend to make guesses or apply simple rules of thumb to help speed up the decision-making process. By understanding how our minds do this, it is possible to position information cleverly in order to push or 'nudge' a choice in a particular direction. This is something that could complement many of your initiatives. In fact, some of these techniques are used very successfully in sales.

You could exploit any of the following seven concepts to your advantage:

1. Anchoring
   When required to estimate something, the introduction of a specific number sets a subconscious starting point or 'anchor' from which figures are either increased or decreased. Believe it or not, this actually affects a person's final choice. For example, if people are asked to make a donation to a charity and the choices offered are £10, £20 or £30... people will give less than if they were offered £20, £40 or £80. This

could be called the 'presumptive sale' or 'presumptive close'. You're presuming that they're going to buy, and are giving a choice on how much they intend to spend.

This is a technique that is also used in negotiation either to raise or lower the opposition's expectations. You could use it to offer the boss input to your client service charter. The choice is how he'd like to phrase the charter, not whether to have one or not.

2. Availability
People tend to assess the likelihood of risk based on how easily similar examples come to mind. People's tendency to purchase insurance cover for natural disasters is higher immediately after such an event. When thinking of death, people think more readily of homicide and often wrongly believe that more people die from homicide than suicide.

While this may sound cynical, there is a particular window just after a crisis. People are more likely to look for ways of avoiding similar crises in the future. You could apply this to staff who've just been bawled out by the boss, or to the boss who's just had poor quarterly results. New insurance policies against earthquake damage always peak just after an earthquake!

3. Representativeness (sorry, their word!)
People believe they can detect patterns which have

great meaning but are, in fact, simple chance. For example, if you flip a coin and it comes up heads three times in a row, most people would be surprised. If you are alert to opportunities, it may be possible to claim success or allow others to believe in the success of something and attribute significance to it – even if this is not the case.

You could use this to build a link between some aspect of the organisation you want to change and link that to something the boss is concerned about. For example, the boss may be concerned about the company's ever-rising phone bill. You could suggest that the company moves to contacting clients by email and text rather than by phone, which would save a huge amount on phone bills as well as reducing the time spent trying to speak to clients. The real benefit to the company might be that this change allows you to develop the internal and external e-communications of the business, which the boss was opposed to, under the guise of reducing the phone bill.

4. Optimism and Overconfidence
   We've already mentioned the fact that people tend to overestimate their abilities and consider themselves to be above average. For example, 40% of marriages end in divorce yet almost no couples getting married believe it will happen to them. If your boss is likely to overestimate his immunity to a risky decision and, consequently, neglects to take

sensible precautions, he may benefit from a 'nudge' where you remind him of how something went wrong recently. The bullying we illustrated in Chapter 7, for example, could be used the next time there's a staff dispute. Jo could remind Brian how his early approach of simply telling people how to behave wasn't very effective. The department now functions much more efficiently after Jo helped Brian to understand the issues, deal with those and repair the relationships.

5. Loss Aversion

   This phenomenon results in a strong desire to continue with the current situation rather than risk losing one's current holdings. You'll remember from Chapter 3 how Charlotte needed to suffer an initial loss of performance in her waterskiing as she learnt to reposition himself on her ski. She was worried about a loss of performance, but was, finally, willing to take the risk in order to improve further.

   For example, you might hold out the possibility of risk or loss if your boss doesn't introduce the service charter. This is not a threat! You're merely using the idea of danger and failure to nudge him in the right direction.

6. *Status Quo* Bias (Inertia)

   People tend to stick with their current situation. For example, when applying for a new driving licence in the UK you now have to consciously 'opt out' of donating your organs. Most people do not bother. This has effectively increased the organ donor pool without any significant action by the general public.

You might use this to include something in your original charter that might not be an obvious fit, but will stay there because it's easier to leave it in than to take it out. For example, you could include a question on what staff say they need to provide great customer service. Just think what doors that might open for you!

7. Framing
You will feel better about a medical procedure when you are told that there is a 95% survival rate, as opposed to the doctor saying there was a 1 in 20 chance of death!

Similarly, your staff will react better if they're told that 80% of top companies use your system of charters than that 1 in 5 of the top companies don't have one.

Before you can start to play any game, however, you want to try to make sure that you are a better player than your rivals. Unfair? Maybe, but this particular game is one you don't want to lose. In the next chapter we'll be looking at some more tips and tricks to add nuance to your game.

You may play sport or, even if you don't, you'll know that it's possible for sportsmen and women to attend clinics where their golf swing, swimming stroke or baseball pitch is analysed using motion capture software. The results allow the coaches to make, often tiny, changes to parts of the movement, which result in great benefits. Simply sitting differently on a bicycle saddle can mean the difference between 'just' winning an Olympic medal and breaking a world record in the process. Or, at the amateur level, between a comfortable bike ride or getting home in agony. Tiny changes can make a big difference in the long-term.

This is what we'll be looking at in more detail in Chapter 10.

10

IMPLEMENTING CHANGE – FINAL CONSIDERATIONS

THE CRUNCHY BIT

Your next step is to take the group of newly-enthused individuals that you've created and bond them together as a team. We've looked at the four different personality types in terms of your boss – you should try to balance your team with the same range of strengths (and weaknesses). While that may create conflict, your team members should now be able to be more accepting of conflicting views as adding depth and new ideas to the discussions.

Your leadership is key in helping the team to work together well. When a diverse group comes together, they will go through Tuckman's classical phases of forming, storming, norming and performing. Don't try to skip steps! This is a normal process on the way to achieving high performing teams – and can even work backwards on occasion. Your role is to keep them in the performing phase as much as possible.

Feedback oils the wheels of change and helps get the team to the next level. This feedback may be positive or negative, and both you and the team should be accepting of it. There will be problems, and problem solving is inherent in what teams do.

As the project of organisational change gains momentum, you'll need more hands to the wheel. That help may come from within the team you're creating or from elsewhere. It's surprising just how willing people are to give help when asked.

Lead by example: ask questions, offer help and undertake ongoing self-improvement. Help might come from other sources, too, and you'll do well to be able to tap into people in positions of authority or influence in the organisation to move change along. The better you understand these power structures in your workplace, the more effectively you'll be able to do this.

STRONGER TOGETHER

An organisation needs to balance client focus, innovation, quality, efficiency and teamwork, among many other considerations. We've discussed the *Good to Great* principles and philosophy. Even being good is a challenge, let alone great! Cameron and Quinn proposed a *Competing Values* framework that is valuable in identifying various management skill sets that need to be balanced in order to ensure long-term success. To be an effective manager, you need to be above average or better across all four of Cameron's quadrants (see our modified version on the next page) and be able to use your strengths well. The more balanced your profile, the better you will be able to integrate capabilities from opposing quadrants. For example, being results-focused gives you a 30% chance of being a leader, whilst a collaborative focus yields only a 9% chance of leadership. However, being able to flex both these capabilities well increases the likelihood of effective leadership to 66%!

Essentially, Cameron's model looks at organisational dynamics from two perspectives: a focus/flexibility scale, and an external/internal focus. We have modified this to include the social styles framework proposed by Wilson Learning, giving our model a related but subtly different set of axes: task/team (i.e. how focused are you on getting the job done at any cost, as opposed to getting everyone to the end of the game even at lower performance levels) and ask/tell (i.e. how much do you tend to ask for input and lead people with their own idea, compared to simply telling them what to do?). The result gives us four quadrants, with the typical Driver (Results Rupert) in the top right corner and the Analyst (Detail Danny) in the top left. Bottom left is the Amiable (Likable Larry), while the Expressive (Excitable Eric) occupies the bottom right. This links clearly to our analysis of the boss in Chapter 2.

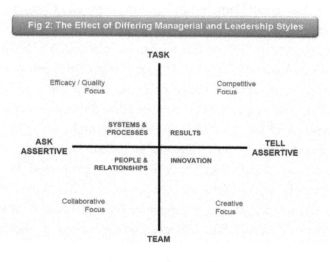

Fig 2: The Effect of Differing Managerial and Leadership Styles

Irrespective of the culture you are trying to develop, it makes sense to ensure that these competencies are adequately balanced within your team. While it is possible for one person to move between all four quadrants effectively, to enhance the likelihood of success you should try to include people whose skills complement one another so that all the bases are covered. Obviously, this can increase the potential for conflict, especially in the diagonally opposing quadrants: the creative/control (expressive/analytical) quadrants and the compete/collaborate (driver/amiable) quadrants.

CONFLICT CAN BE GOOD

By now, if you have done your job well, people should see conflict in a more positive light or at least able to utilise systems and process better to ensure that conflicting energies are channelled appropriately. The ideal is actually to value differences – which in an alternative culture could easily lead to conflict.

Jo's very intrigued by developments in the copy department. It seems like only yesterday that she was coaching Brian on how to handle the conflicts and bullying that were taking place there. The team didn't gel at all and were constantly bickering and fighting.

Now, however, the copy department seems not only to be a model of calm and happiness, they have actually started coming forward with ways to cut costs and to look for external business to keep the writers busy in quiet times at Simian. They have even brought in business from American and Australian agencies who appreciate the department's attention to detail!

The team hasn't changed during this time. But what's happened is that they have learnt to use the different strengths and talents available to them to best advantage. Mel, the department head is still extremely expressive, and two of her staff, including Sarah, are amiable but, instead of them being intimidated by her outbursts, they now see them as passion and commitment that allow her to excel creatively.

Jo is both amazed and delighted – and so is Brian!

FROM HERE TO THERE (AND BACK?)

Indeed, Bruce Tuckman's Team Development Model is very useful in helping people in newly-formed or still-forming groups to position conflict positively as a natural part of the group's development and functioning. Tuckman sees the typical sequence of group development as passing through four phases: 'forming, storming, norming and performing'.

During the **forming** phase, groups are involved in defining interpersonal and task behaviour. When the copy department recruits a new member, the team has to form again and redefine roles.

The **storming** phase is characterised by conflict and polarisation with regard to interpersonal questions, which results in task-focused behaviour. This manifested as bullying in the copy department, where the staff were unable to see their boss' behaviour as anything other than aggressive – while she thought they weren't nearly passionate enough!

The **norming** phase is reached when the group begins to resolve conflicts and create new standards and roles, as well as group cohesion and feelings of group attachment. Brian's work, amazingly to Jo, really helped the department in this. They began to recognise that their head was truly passionate about her work while she saw that getting along didn't mean working to an inferior standard.

In the **performing** phase, the interpersonal relationships facilitate the achievement of group goals. People are more flexible and activities are focused on the execution of the group task. This is the current state of our friends in the copy department – harmonious efficiency and teamwork.

It is clear that group development is a complex process. Development depends on the type of group, the environment within which the group operates, its aims and other factors. All groups do not move through the same development phases, and some disintegrate before they reach the final phase. Some phases are abbreviated in certain groups, while others may occur more than once. In general, however, we can say that most groups develop according to the phases described by Tuckman. These phases can be displayed in either direction: it is possible to move from norming back to storming, for example, and the introduction of a new challenge or external pressure can frequently cause this 'backwards' step to occur. Don't be afraid of this: accept that new challenges will bring new pressures, and new ways must be found to deal with them. The group members should not feel threatened if they recognise what is going on.

We have highlighted the fact that a poor performer often tends not to accurately assess his performance levels. This has to be managed very carefully as you may be able to develop an ally who, while very committed to the cause, lacks the necessary skill to help progress matters further. The easiest option would be to channel his efforts into areas where his greatest competencies lie. It is possible, however, that you could end up in a situation where he is unable to help you despite his best intentions. As there is no direct or formal management system in place for dealing with this you need a timely positive intervention.

DIFFERENT STROKES FOR DIFFERENT FOLKS

In cases such as this, appropriate feedback is probably one of the most important and powerful tools at your disposal. Providing such feedback is always difficult but, if it's constructive, you not only get the message across but also build a more cohesive and capable team.

Jo's seen these 'keen but green' folk before. They're all fired up by some part of the vision, but tend to go off on their own tangents. Keeping them aligned with her plan is difficult and, because she's often not their line manger, she doesn't have many opportunities to guide them. Getting the feedback right in the little time she might have with each one is critical, and she's unsure of the best way forward.

Constructive feedback is an important way to help people learn and develop – both personally and professionally. The correct application of this technique enables you to give honest yet robust messages. However, instead of insulting, shutting-down or alienating people (thereby lowering their morale and productivity), constructive feedback motivates them to ask for help and acknowledge a skill or competency deficiency, while feeling supported and respected. Constructive feedback, when delivered out of respect and a genuine desire for the individual to improve, accomplishes two of the most important factors influencing employee retention and satisfaction: the feeling of having a great boss, and being part of a team. Providing feedback in this way enables you to build the competence and cohesion of your team, while effectively managing performance issues. It also enables you to remain respected, well liked and considered 'a great boss'.

As a guiding principle it is worth remembering that while criticism works well, praise works better. A balanced approach works best of all. To get the balance right you are advised to structure your feedback making sure the following aspects are all adequately addressed:

- Timing is all – if undesirable traits are not corrected timeously, people may unknowingly incorporate them it into their standard behaviour. 'Unlearning' things is very difficult

- Monitor your body language and make sure that you remain assertive
- Look out for defensive body language in others and adjust your approach appropriately
- Focus on specific, objective facts rather than opinion and hearsay
- Stick to a few key points, preferably just one or two
- Have a nice, clear opening statement that sets the agenda. "I'm disappointed," or, "I was really pleased by," are effective openings, for example
- Have a logical order to the discussion and prioritise issues
- You need some elements of praise (making sure that this does not overshadow the negative issue you have to address)
- Where possible, turn negatives into positives. (e.g. turning problems into learning opportunities)
- Invite the individual receiving the feedback to share his perspective or provide his response
- First ask for suggestions and ideas before offering any of your own
- Remember to complete the 'learning loop' and praise people when they take feedback on board and show more of the desired behaviours.

When reprimanding 'winners', linking the feedback to praise is especially motivating for them and is likely to increase their levels of motivation to apply corrective action. For example, you might say that the person you're talking to has always performed a particular task exceptionally well, which makes it even more disappointing to find a problem this time.

For 'learners' the most tactful approach could be to look at revising their learning goals. For example, you might say that you, the mentor, have been mistaken in setting the goals too high and that you now want to concentrate on smaller, more achievable steps or stages. You might dress this up as harnessing the learner's enthusiasm in cementing incremental improvements.

The generally-accepted rule is to praise people at least five times more than often than you criticise them. Praise is most effective when given as soon as possible after the event. Immediate positive feedback helps reinforce the desired behaviour – making a recurrence more likely (see successive approximation, Chapter 3).

DO AS I DO

We have emphasised the importance of leading by example. It is important that you not only improve your skills and techniques at giving feedback, but that you improve your skills and abilities at *receiving* feedback.

We suggest you should:

- Regularly and frequently ask for feedback
- Express your desire to improve. By outlining areas you could improve in, you increase the likelihood of people giving you useful and detailed feedback
- Gather opinion from all perspectives. Keep an eye out

for any themes that appear to be developing – these are priority areas for attention!

- Demonstrate an interest in what's being said. Use active listening, open body language, questioning, taking notes and summarising to check for understanding

- Focus on hearing what is being said and not what you expect to hear – avoid the temptation to explain yourself as this can sound defensive. Explore what positive actions you can take as a result. Knowing what behaviours you should build on can be more effective than attempting to change what isn't working. In other words, make what you're good at even better rather than trying to make your particular weakness stronger – unless that weakness is critical to your success. As an example, let's say you're great with people and mediocre with numbers. Spending time on your people skills could make you one of the best in the business, while spending time on your numeracy will not bring any real benefits to the work that you do

- Say thank you! If you are seen to welcome feedback, you'll receive more and thereby increase your opportunities for self improvement.

At all stages of this project you are likely to be presented with situations that require you to ask others for help. Early on, this is more likely to help you to get your systems and processes started. With time, there will be some momentum developed and your interventions will be aimed at helping to steer the project in the right direction or to get complementary projects off the ground. Whatever the situation, your ability to ask for help can be a defining feature in the levels of support you get for this project.

JUST ASK

Professor Francis Flynn has done groundbreaking work in this area and we would like to highlight some important conclusions for you here. We would recommend you look at the YouTube clip *If you need something just ask* from the Stanford Graduate School of Business, www.youtube.com/watch?v=HcVFJCNa4ak.

In this short film, people hugely underestimate the likelihood of others helping them in response to a request. This is because they tend to focus more on the costs of saying yes and seldom consider that the person being asked is more likely to consider what are the costs of saying no. We tend to assume automatically that, since the request requires additional effort on behalf of the other person, it will result in their refusal. In fact, people are more likely to be thinking about how difficult it is for them to say no or how bad they are likely to feel or look as a result of their saying no.

This effect can be altered by changing the type of request, the way the request is made and the context within which the request is made. Irrespective of this, studies conducted by Professor Flynn show that people tend to overestimate levels of refusal by as much as 50% to 100%. What is also interesting is that 20% of the people who were asked to participate in the study refused to do so because they felt they would not get help from the people they asked. This means that the group that did participate in the study were more optimistic about their chances of eliciting help from others. However, despite this optimism they still greatly underestimated the likelihood of people doing simple things to help them like answering a questionnaire, letting them use their cellular phones or escorting them to a local gymnasium.

Another interesting feature of these studies was that there did not appear to be a difference in the rate of refusal when asking friends and family compared with asking complete strangers! Even successful charity fundraisers, when asked to estimate their success rates, showed the same high levels of underestimation.

Another significant finding is that the size of the request did not significantly alter the likelihood of people saying yes. What was important was the way people were asked. Direct personal requests (i.e. requests made face to face) were more likely to be agreed to irrespective of how difficult the request was, but indirect requests (i.e. making the same request via email) were 50% less likely to get a positive response. This is critical for you because if you want to maximise the likelihood of people helping you – *you need to ask them directly!*

Surprisingly, if people had previously denied a request for help, they were more likely to say yes to a second request for help. We know this is counterintuitive but you should not to ignore these findings. This can help your project gain significant momentum.

To increase the likelihood of compliance we can add a 'nudge'. Professor Flynn quotes a study where the success rate of help given increased from 54% to 87% simply by adding the words *"Would you do me a favour?"* before the request was made.

JUST ASK!

We also tend to overestimate how likely people are to ask for help if they are struggling with something. Apparently, we can't predict accurately just how awkward it is for people to ask for assistance when they are having difficulty. That causes us to undervalue what we have to offer. To increase the likelihood of people asking for help, we need to help them to focus on what the benefits are rather than simply making ourselves available to help. You need to be acutely aware of this because you don't want your converts losing momentum and enthusiasm purely because you assume they will ask for help when they are struggling. This phenomenon also has particular relevance to your role as a coach, and the role of others, too.

A final point that may also prove useful in converting people to your cause, or at least softening their attitude towards you: Professor Flynn found that when people did not initially want to help but then did, the act of helping increased their likelihood of being more favourably predisposed to the person they had helped!

NOT ALL LEADERS WEAR 'LEADER' BADGES

You may feel that you don't have the authority to implement some of the changes you'd like to make. In *Lateral Leadership,* Fisher and Sharp have a method of comparing the things that you can do without authority to those you can do with authority. Outside of making decisions that no-one else can and ordering people to do things, the lists are identical! By ensuring you are good at all the other parts of the job, there is every likelihood that you will need to give very few orders – even if you could. Also, if you think back on everything we've said so far, would it really be wise for you as the boss to routinely and regularly be making decisions without the input and support of the significant players on the team? Let's look at the things Fisher and Sharp feel can improve the way you and your colleagues get things done together:

Improving your personal skills
- Creating a climate of mutual support and feedback
- Becoming engaged in challenging tasks
- Carrying out regular reviews and learning from experience
- Solving problems
- Having clarity of purpose in terms of clearly-formulated results.

Working towards organisational goals
- Asking good questions

- Offering help e.g. data, ideas, suggestions or advice
- Setting an example

Remaining open to different and potentially better ideas from others with whom you work.

Consider that power is traditionally understood within the context of a Control Culture (we have described four differing types of organisational cultures – each with power manifesting in different ways). In competence cultures, power manifests as expertise. Relationships and charisma are manifestations of power in collaborative and cultivation cultures, respectively.

By now you will be well aware that discussions, decisions and arguments within organisations do not depend on logic alone. We hope to have convinced you that decisions depend as much upon emotional considerations as they do on facts. Since power is rarely equally divided in any group, some people's opinions will carry more weight. This is a power source that needs to be recognised in order to be fully utilised and exploited. Some people have power because of the position that they hold.

Your boss may be a good example of this. Understanding how he got there is probably as valuable as the power he presently wields by virtue of his position. Positions of influence within an organisation can vary. A comprehensive understanding of the unique dynamic at play within your organisation is essential in planning your way forward.

WHO'S GOT THE POWER?

Management Learning & Coaching Ltd's Online Academy provides a very useful outline of different positions of influence:

- Network – excellent contacts which are a ready source of information and support
- Political – an understanding of who can help or hinder the progress of a project, plan or idea and how to get their support
- Process – a detailed and thorough understanding of organisational systems and processes
- Role – influence by virtue of their position and/or function
- Safe Hands – careful, responsible, dependable and reliable when given something to do
- Expertise – technical know-how, be that scientific, process or professional
- Leadership – the ability to motivate and create followers
- Creativity – the ability to be inventive, innovative and see things through
- Market – in-depth knowledge of industry developments, trends and practices
- Customers – strong relationships with external customers together with the knowledge and understanding of what they will or are likely to think.

By expanding your personal levels of influence and gaining

the support of others with complementary areas, you will increase your ability to progress a project. However, exerting some kinds of influence may come more easily to you than other kinds. We recommend that you work on expanding your area of influence by looking at the sway you presently have and identifying activities that are closely related to this. For example, if you are reasonably influential politically, then working on networking will probably be rather easy.

When influencing your boss, keeping any level of control can be a tricky business. Power-hungry controllers need a lot of help to understand that processes can be just as important as outcomes. If we rush towards what appears to us to be a self-evident end point without involving others in the journey, we risk alienating them from outcomes they may have wanted. The effort and energy now required merely to justify that end point usually will, at best, result in grudging acquiescence. Remember that no-one wins when you win an argument with a customer – even if they are internal customers! You lose trust and commitment, there's a negative effect on the emotional bank balance.

We have warned that weak relationships could result in poor communication, tension, disagreement, jealousy, back-biting and criticism. As the power balance changes and the tipping point is passed, make sure that care is taken to invest in your relationship with your boss. This is important for others to do as well. Remind people that the boss is also an internal customer and consistency is essential if you are all truly to embrace this value system.

Unless you are aiming for a coup, your boss has value to add and can help give momentum by supporting the project. However, this is less likely to happen if he has been alienated during the revolution.

If you are dealing with a conservative late-adopter, look for sources that he respects against which he can benchmark himself and the organisation. The sources of reference for this need not necessarily be successful competitors. You may find that your late adopter looks to what he considers a successful organisation or team that is totally unrelated to your sector. The key thing is that, for him, their credibility is high and the relevant practices they adopt are seen as part of the reason for their success. If you have evidence of successful initiatives there's no shame in *boldly following where others lead* – as long as it gets the organisation moving in the right direction. Incidentally this approach is also very useful in helping to cope with a person whose primary fear is one of failure. By helping them see that the approach resulted in success, you may be able to nudge them into adopting this practice in your organisation.

DON'T HOLD YOUR BREATH FOR THANKS

Another area that requires a little practice is finding the delicate balance between publicising your successes (which risks undermining your boss' credibility, image or authority) and helping your boss gain sufficient confidence in your ability to overcome his inherent fear of failure.

This fear may be related to his lack of involvement in a specific project or task. There is a strong likelihood that by directly exercising power, influence and control your boss receives some form of direct feedback affirming his indispensability. Over time, with repeated hints and by setting a successful example, you should aim to nudge your boss towards an understanding that this power and control is surpassed when people take ownership and responsibility without his direction.

A MODEL FOR THE MANAGEMENT OF CHANGE

THE CRUNCHY BIT

It is often hard to tell that change is happening. When you're swimming in the sea, it is very easy to get swept away in the current without realising what's going on. You can't feel the current you're in, but you look back to shore and suddenly realise how far you've gone!

There are two kinds of change to consider. Top-down change is usually planned, with systems and processes put into place to support it. It can take time for the people in the organisation to adapt to it, however.

Bottom-up change is less planned and often 'just happens', with systems developing organically to support it. Here, it takes time for the official systems to adapt to the change. Of course, you may play a role in that 'just happens' process…

For change to take place, you'll need to overcome fear of change and the status quo. You'll need dissatisfaction with that status quo, a shared vision of the future and enough people to change their behaviours in order to overcome any resistance. It's often the case that pushing someone harder simply causes them to push back harder! Results may be easier to obtain by reducing resistance to change, rather than forcing someone down a road he or she's afraid to start on.

Once you've got the change started, it gains momentum quickly. Ensure that support structures and other resources are in place to maintain that change, as well as learning what to prioritise and what to delegate to others – or simply to ignore!

Jo feels she's made some good progress. She's taken the trouble to work out what makes Brian tick. She now knows how to present information to him in a way that allows him to hear her better. She's getting good reports from people in the organisation who seem to share her ideas of how Simian could evolve. She's pretty sure that they're on her side.

Brian seems to have changed his own style as a result of her prompting. He's more likely to ask for opinions and seems to listen when they're offered. He's even started to talk about giving more ownership of decisions to his staff!

DO YOU BELIEVE IN DÉJÀ VU?
DO YOU BELIEVE IN DÉJÀ VU?
(DO YOU SEE WHAT WE DID THERE?)

But, on a day-to-day basis, there seems to be a lot of talk with very little action. Brian's still very much the man in charge for all major decisions, and most minor ones are also brought to him.

So, while Jo's pleased with the overall tone and direction that Simian seems to be moving in, it all seems terribly, terribly slow. She's been hard at work for eight months, day and (often) night, pushing them along with all her might and, as far as tangible results go, there seems precious little to show for her efforts. She's frustrated. Again!

> Jerry is supportive. "Jo," he says, "it's just a matter of reaching a tipping point. All the pieces are in place. Momentum is slow, but it's all in the right direction and it's building up. Once you reach that point, you'll be amazed at how quickly things can change! When Charlotte learnt to waterski, don't you remember how frustrated she was to start with? You kept encouraging her and, once she'd finally got up, she got better really quickly. Really quickly! It was slow to start with and then faster and faster. Don't you think that's what's happening here?"

TOP-DOWN OR BOTTOM-UP?

Many organisations force change: senior management makes decisions which are rolled out across the business. In many cases there is a lag phase where the upper echelons of the organisation have 'moved on' with much of the team still operating under the old paradigm (Fig 3).

In essence, what we are suggesting here is that you effect change in exactly the opposite way to that illustrated in Figure 3 i.e. you work on the lower echelons and

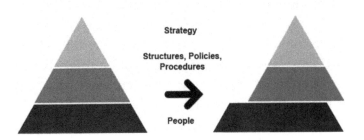

Fig 3: Planned Strategic Change with a "Lag" Phase

Strategy

Structures, Policies, Procedures

People

gradually get them to move ahead of those above them. Especially if this process includes middle and some upper management, there is a degree of inevitability in the 'leaders' also following the 'herd' (Chapter 8, Fig 1).

As we said in Chapter 3, any organisation's objectives and working arrangements will change over time as demands and objectives change. This is usually a passive and gradual form of change and is evolutionary in its development.

Early evolutionary change is often slow and uncertain, and takes place before you reach a tipping point. In order to harness this process to your own ends, it is advisable to explore all the factors leading to change and their interrelationships. This analysis helps identify those processes which are the most useful. With a good understanding of the factors leading to change and the processes involved, the chances of unforeseen outcomes is reduced. The intended result can thus be achieved with a fair degree of certainty.

A RECIPE AT LAST!

When dissatisfaction with the *status quo*, a shared vision of the future and achievable action points overcome organisational inertia, the process moves forward. As Jerry said with reference to the tipping point, you can expend a lot of effort in reaching this point, but change happens very quickly once that point is reached.

A useful equation (originally proposed by community health practitioners Ebrahim and Ranken) illustrates this point:

Change occurs when (A + B + C) > D – and not before.

A – dissatisfaction with the *status quo*. This includes inadequate planning, poor morale, disempowerment, hidden agendas or an unsustainable profit imperative.
B – a shared vision of a brighter future.
C – action plans and practical steps.
D – inertia and the fear of change.

This is the model for the management of change, as well as implementing it. It's no good knowing the path if you don't actually follow it. Dissatisfaction has to be real, coaching has to be effective and the action plans and practical steps need to be achievable and, ideally, non-threatening. Non-threatening can't be to the point of not changing things at all! There is always an element of challenge, big or small, with change. The key is not to make any step too challenging or you'll risk a backlash.

Jo's journey gives us a lovely, concrete example, as Jerry has just reminded her. There is undoubtedly great inertia at Simian. People were very used to the *status quo* and Brian was very used to being the man in charge. The levels of achievement of Simian in creative terms were truly surprising, given the degree of disempowerment present. What Jo has done over her eight brief months with the company is to bring to the surface her colleagues' dissatisfaction with the *status quo* (A). In addition, as we've seen, she's provided coaching towards a shared vision. She's taken a lot of time to talk to her colleagues and co-workers and has created a common language and vision for the future (B). She is engaged now in proposing her plan for change (C). This includes simple, non-threatening, practical steps that people can take to help move Simian inexorably towards that tipping point, where A + B + C will overcome D, the organisation's resistance to change, its inertia.

It's important to bear in mind that the leadership, as well as the staff, can be dissatisfied with the *status quo*. Brian's morale might also be affected by Jo showing him how things could be different and better. By widening the perceived gap between where Brian is currently and where he might be in the better, brighter future, he'll be more inclined to support the forces for change.

Inertia is the primary force to be overcome in order for change to take place.

In fossilising organisations, the tendency is for people and systems simply to run on, as if on rails.

Change is actively resisted as it threatens to take people out of their comfort zones or to deprive them of their power.

In order for this inertia to be overcome, it must be overwhelmed by the combination of A, B and C, above.

FIRST THINGS FIRST

Initially, you are likely to be the only resource that you have at your disposal. As your campaign begins to gain momentum, you may be able to call on other resources to assist in progressing matters or dealing with crises. Either way, given that you still have to fulfil your primary role or function within the organisation, it is essential to ensure that you prioritise and focus your efforts.

Stephen Covey suggests that we should first deal with true problems and crises, then focus on the things that, if left unattended for any significant period, will escalate into crises. These are the mission-critical activities which, if properly attended to, will yield firm foundations and are likely to result in the development of future opportunities. Finally, look at issues which may appear pressing but, in reality, may have very little impact on the grand scheme of things. Prioritisation can be enhanced by building a simple table: important to less important on one axis and urgent to less urgent on the other. Only those things that are both important and urgent should receive your immediate attention.

Urgent and Important matters are crises and must be dealt with immediately. Examples include production line breakdowns, a fire in a warehouse or a critical sales meeting in two minutes' time! Failing to attend to these high-level priorities will have an immediate detrimental effect on the business.

Non-urgent but important matters would include planning and strategy meetings, examining the strategies of your competitors, or your own exercise and relaxation. If these matters are not attended to they will result in crises developing. While not urgent, this group is *by far the most important* if you want to make your organisation great.

Urgent but not important matters are the cold callers, the newspaper that's just landed on your desk and other general distractions. Covey usefully calls these 'other people's problems'!

Finally, there is the **Non-urgent and not important** group: the colour scheme for the staff toilets, which binding to use for old newspapers and other general trivia and junk. There is never any reason to deal with these – except, perhaps, if you have completely run out of anything else to do and are bored!

REDUCING RESISTANCE

The following are examples of resistance to change and ways of reducing it, based on the revealing work by Ebrahim and Ranken.

Reasons for resistance	Ways to reduce resistance to change
Fear of the unknown	Use of consultation, seminars, discussion papers, workshops, selling your vision, coaching and enabling, focusing on the 'pain' of the *status quo*, motivating towards the 'pleasure' to be had in a new paradigm, leading by example, being inspirational, choice architecture, empowerment strategies, use of a framework for systematic thinking
Loss of existing privilege	Demonstrate that change will enhance or maintain existing status or recompense for loss of privilege or status in other ways, e.g. increased profit, greater kudos, etc.
Imposed by someone else	Look for decisions by consensus and encourage those likely to be affected to produce solutions
Too complicated	Keep all new procedures

	simple and make
	adequate time available
	for training and transition
Increased committee work	Reduce the number of
	committees and the
	duration of their
	meetings
Threat to security, values and	Regular opportunities to
ideals	spread information
	rationally
Greater likelihood of mistakes	Enable aspirations and
	expectations to be
	articulated

It is surprising what patience, time, skill, openness and emphasising the positive can do to create a shared vision. Even failure need not be a major setback. If every attempt at change is used as a learning exercise, then failures can be used to improve the design and to do better in the future, gaining momentum as you go.

By facilitating group formation around the cause that you have all embraced, you can guide movement towards a point beyond which change is irreversible – even by the boss. You will need to ensure that the new group dynamics don't result in the wrong decisions being made. A group can, for example, be a good way of abdicating individual responsibility as we'll see in the next chapter.

Focus on soft rather than hard issues (values, ethos and culture rather than mission, vision, strategies and plans) and avoid positional negotiation on any relevant change-related issue with the boss or Powerful Others.

By engaging with and involving people early in the process, you can develop and motivate them in anticipation of the desired changes. In winning over hearts and minds (by example, by persuasion and by being inspirational), you help people to see, feel and believe that they can make a difference.

By managing and setting their expectations you help in sustaining high levels of motivation, in part by projecting positivity. You should make regular use of feedback to elicit support, help people to learn and develop and to maintain focus and perspective.

Jo feels somewhat reassured. Now that Jerry's put this all into perspective, she's able to see that she really is a long way along the path. In fact, she can recognise her feelings from Chapter 7.
What Jerry's done is to recognise her as in need of both direction and support – both of which he's provided!

She recognises her journey has been a long one and, while the tipping point may not yet have been reached, further progress along this path will inevitably bring success.

The tipping point is a very important idea, to which we'll now turn in Chapter 12.

12
IMPLEMENTING CHANGE – MOVING TOWARDS THE TIPPING POINT

THE CRUNCHY BIT

Overnight success is usually years in the making! Most of these success stories are the result of years of hard work and preparation. Momentum takes time to build up but, once you reach a certain rate of change, progress seems to take on a life of its own. As change gathers speed and passes the tipping point, it's all you can do to keep it moving in the right direction by nudging it when it starts to move off course.

In the early phases of gathering pace, you need to know who to talk to and how to make your message as resonant to them as possible, in the context in which they're operating. As the process continues and new ideas take root, contribution to change passes from the individual worker to groups. But beware the dangers of group working: it's all too easy for a group to dilute out responsibility or to succumb to 'groupthink'.

Throughout the process of change, you'll need to inspire, lead, sell your ideas to others, mentor and coach – and all by influence rather than control. The focus here is on empowerment to allow others to take on responsibility.

It's well worth stopping to check your progress from time to time so that you can discover whether you're on track and if you've gone astray. Do this and plan any corrective action consciously and systematically. Lots of momentum is great, but only if it's in the right direction!

THE TIPPING POINT - AT LAST!

Jo's frustration at the slow pace of change is completely understandable. It's common to feel annoyed when you put a great deal of effort into something and then have to wait for what feels like ages for only small gains. As Jerry pointed out at the end of the last chapter, however, this is a common pattern.

If you follow our advice, plan carefully and then consistently follow through, you will see things starting to change. You can then watch change gather pace. Just as Jim Collins saw with the great companies, there will be a gradual increase in momentum until eventually, with just a bit of luck, the project will take on a life of its own. At this stage your role will change from getting things moving to ensuring that the appropriate focus remains and keeping the project on track.

Malcolm Gladwell researched this extensively in his book *The Tipping Point.* Gladwell insightfully suggests that ideas, messages, behaviours and trends tend to follow patterns of spread, similar to those of infectious agents in an epidemic. He proposes that behaviours or ideas can be 'contagious'. A number of small changes have an increasingly significant effect until eventually there is a dramatic moment, the *'Tipping Point'*, when matters move forward much more rapidly than before, and with a degree of inevitability – no matter what the boss thinks. The organisation will have shifted beneath him.

A good recent example of this is the rise of social media. Facebook, Twitter and other social networks are only a few years old. At first, they were regarded as gimmicks. Their growth was slow but steady until the tipping point was reached. Now, for an adult not to have a Facebook account or be active on social media (as one of the authors confesses not to be) is unusual to the point of comment.

From an external perspective, the observed changes appeared to be dramatic breakthroughs, but, for the insider, they were more properly perceived as an organic development process. *Outliers*, Malcolm Gladwell's study of overnight success, shows the same dynamic operating. The basic premise relates to how you need to 'do your time', learning the intricacies and quirks of any job before you can achieve mastery. Or, in Gladwell's terms, to become an expert at anything you need to spend 10,000 hours doing it. This, of course, is necessary but may not be sufficient! But the bottom line is not to expect anything to happen overnight, and sometimes even masses of hard work may not be enough!

Let's look at an example that the authors are particularly familiar with: the laboratory growth of bacteria. Start with a bacterial culture plate and place a small group of bacteria onto it. The bacteria need a bit of time to acclimatise to the medium and get into the swing of things. Growth is slow, almost invisible. This is what is called the 'lag phase' of growth and, while there is growth, it is not very rapid. Incidentally, contrary to popular opinion, this is the reason why early treatment with antibiotics is a good thing. The likelihood of a good result is far greater when there are not many bacteria and they are not growing wildly. Over a period of time, the growth on the plate also reaches a tipping point and then moves into what is called the 'log phase' where growth is so rapid it is no longer arithmetic but rather logarithmic. The bugs fill the plate as if overnight.

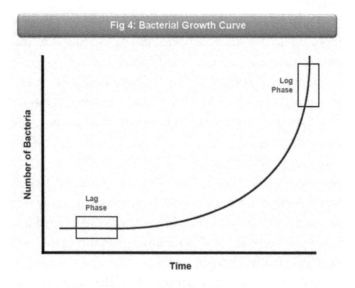

Fig 4: Bacterial Growth Curve

In his analysis of how ideas and trends follow this pattern, Gladwell identifies three key factors: the law of the few, the stickiness factor and the power of context.

The **law of the few** refers to how some people are more important than others in helping matters to reach a tipping point. Gladwell identifies three key types.

Connectors are people who know lots of other people. You will have heard of the theory of *Six Degrees of Separation*. This proposes that if you look hard enough you can get from any person to any other through a maximum of six connected people. For example, I know my university professor of physics, he taught at MIT, the head of department at MIT was previously at the University of Chicago, his best friend taught law – to Barack Obama! That's from me to the President of the United States of America in only five steps – I had one remaining! This is because at least one of those people (my professor of physics) was someone who was well connected and knew many other people. Make sure you know who these people are in the organisation: they can be very useful allies.

Mavens are socially motivated and just love helping people by giving them information. When someone wants to know something specific, he will often look until he has found a trustworthy maven. Don't overlook these people as they will gladly share many of the benefits of your cause with anyone who wants to know. Walking, talking, singing, dancing, free word-of-mouth advertising! Gandhi was a great maven, helping and informing others throughout his life.

Salesmen exude energy, enthusiasm, charm and likeability. While the mavens may be fonts of knowledge, the salesmen are the people who will get you recruits and converts. Tony Blair was regarded by many as a great salesman, irrespective of whether you agreed with his policies or not.

The **stickiness factor** refers to how the message or idea has to 'stick' in your mind i.e. it should be easy to grasp conceptually and easy to remember. While the messengers play an important role in the spread of the message, the content is also very important. The packaging is also essential. This is why you need to prepare what you want to say, to whom you want to say it and, where possible, when you want to say it. Make sure you have identified your customers, profiled them properly and know what their levels of interest are. The better you understand your audience and the more relevant your message is to them, the better it will stick.

Words are important, but never overlook the powerful messages that are conveyed by actions. This is why you need to be mindful of the example you set personally as we shall soon see.

Gladwell cites numerous examples of good ideas failing to take hold purely because the context (or paradigm) in which information was presented was not conducive to its spread. This is called the **power of context**. Be mindful of group dynamics e.g. peer pressure and social norms. Make sure you are as sensitive as possible to when, where and how you present your case. It's no good trying to have a discussion about renewing the sign above the door while the building's on fire. You need to choose your moment.

Remember what we said earlier in this chapter about

stickiness: to make a difference, you need not only to present information or knowledge, but must also be aware of people's attitudes and behaviour if you really want to effect a change in the *status quo*.

CONFORM WITH CARE

As you recruit more and more staff to the cause there will be a tendency to form a group or a number of groups. To a large extent this can serve a very useful function and will play an important role in moving matters closer to your personal organisational tipping point.

Not everything about groups, however, is necessarily positive. As we said at the beginning of the chapter, as momentum builds your role will switch from trying to get things moving (i.e. dealing with organisational and individual inertia) to ensuring that the appropriate focus and direction is maintained. As the cause begins to take on a life of its own it's worth bringing some of the potential negative effects of groups to your attention. Early identification of anything that might lead to these phenomena is vital as, without formal position or power, you will find it very difficult to arrest these processes once they take hold.

The three processes we believe you need to be mindful of are deindividuation, groupthink and the risky-shift phenomenon.

Deindividuation (ghastly word!) refers to the process of losing one's individuality through becoming subsumed into a group. As a result, group members lose their inhibitions or restraints and feel free to engage in negative or destructive behaviour they would normally never display. A perfectly nice person in the presence of a bully will often display bullying behaviour, too, when they would not do so if the bully was absent.

Normally, individual and group behaviour is designed to maximise positive outcomes and minimise negative ones. Therefore people will tend not to carry out activities if they expect group members to disapprove. In the case of deindividuation, the anonymity of a group lessens the possibility of disapproval. Even if there is a negative response, the individual believes that the diffusion of responsibility amongst members will greatly reduce the negative reaction directed at him. Deindividuation is further encouraged by social facilitation: if others behave in a normally disapproved-of way, the degree of restraint on any individual's own behaviour is lessened. The behaviour of others may also create the impression that group norms have changed and that a new form of destructive behaviour has now become acceptable.

Groupthink results in the deterioration of intellectual effectiveness, reality testing and moral convictions due to pressure from within the group. Group members strive so hard for solidarity and cohesion that questions or topics that might lead to differences of opinion are avoided. A great example is the Borg from *Star Trek*. They are all assimilated into the Collective, and resistance is futile. Trying to get a Borg to display human emotion is impossible and irrelevant – unless it's Seven of Nine, of course.

Groupthink is characterised by overwhelming pressure

towards group conformity. Differences of opinion even concerning relatively minor issues are not well tolerated. In some cases harsh action is taken against dissenters or members who criticise group decisions. With groupthink there is a tendency for group members to suppress their discomfort with certain group decisions. Some members act as selective filters by keeping controversial information away from the group.

Groupthink is further characterised by the illusion that the group's plans are practically foolproof. Decision-makers believe their actions are morally defensible, and take a stance of the end justifying the means. Group members are also inclined to avoid or minimize information opposing their decision and place greater importance on data supporting their position.

Not all groups are equally vulnerable to groupthink. It would seem that:

- highly cohesive groups have a higher tendency to discuss things. This does not necessarily imply that they encourage dissent, though
- impartial leadership may decrease the likelihood of groupthink. Especially if member input and the discussion of alternatives is encouraged.
- leaders can help by avoiding the expression of their own preferred solution as this tends to limit critical analysis and increases the likelihood that the group will adopt this decision as its final choice
- a more insular group will generate and evaluate fewer alternatives.

Research suggests that decisions from group-centred groups can be riskier than those taken by leader-centred groups or, indeed, than those that would be taken by the group members individually. Sociologists call this the **Risky Shift Phenomenon**. This would suggest the importance of discussion in the manifestation of this phenomenon. Possible explanations include:

- Group members hoping to elevate their status by demonstrating their willingness to run greater than ordinary risks
- The opinion of the riskiest individual does appear to impact significantly on the group decision
- A group decision may also diffuse individual responsibility, thereby lessening the impact of adverse consequences on any particular individual.

Groups are not bad things! They can allow engagement, encourage ideas to be shared and developed, create or enhance relationships between team members and develop solutions to problems. The drawbacks listed above, while real, are not a reason to stick with an all-powerful leader. Rather, they illustrate potential pitfalls to guard against.

We can now expand on some of the themes covered earlier, and introduce a few additional concepts.

CARRYING THE FLAME

The three key ideas in marketing your plans are leading by

example and being inspirational; selectively and timeously selling your idea; and the relevant training of your staff (including the use of successive approximation).

It is important to realise that real managers have leadership responsibility and need to **lead by example**. This involves doing things right (supervision) and doing the right things (strategy). Failure to do both parts well will see you slip into a purely administrative role, with the focus simply on getting things done.

This redirection of your time into planning, organising and controlling won't allow you to demonstrate the leadership that distinguishes managers from administrators. In the worst-case scenario you could end up being a bureaucrat!

We have talked about some of the likely reasons for a lack of team spirit or low morale. We suggested that there is often a tendency for bean counters to undervalue human resources and favour physical and financial assets. Conventional wisdom is clear that of these three assets, human resources are the most valuable. They determine how the other two assets can be deployed. As the organisation becomes more complex, the human element becomes increasingly important. This is often overlooked because earlier processes and systems were adequate at that earlier stage, and until recently, failed to highlight the relative importance of people.

The most easily overlooked aspect of the human asset in an organisation is relationships. Weak relationships cause poor communication, tension, disagreement, jealousy, back-biting and criticism. These drain time, energy and resources that might otherwise be turned to profit and personal fulfilment. You are unlikely to be able to deal with every single issue that presents itself but, using the approach we will shortly outline, you can start by dealing with this issue not only through action but interaction, which is both more subtle and more complicated. In your priority areas, deal with issues promptly, but do prioritise them so that you don't become overwhelmed. A matrix of the sort described by Stephen Covey in *The 7 Habits of Highly Effective People,* and outlined in Chapter 11, can be very useful.

Where possible, remember to sell this concept to potential allies as they deal with crises that have resulted from neglect of this area. You will recall our statement that you need to see objections as a sign of involvement. It is important to apply a similar perspective when it comes to relationship problems. Add this to the customer service dimension we discussed previously. When people have a problem, in time the problem becomes less of an issue but the way it was handled will be remembered. Relationship problems are opportunities to repair and build bridges between people, and to redefine their roles. And if the relationship is good, the staff will happily go the extra mile for each other and for the customer. That will make the boss happy!

Aspire to lead by influence and not by control. Stephen Covey, in *The 7 Habits of Highly Effective People*, introduces the very useful metaphor of an 'emotional bank account' representing the level of trust that has been built up in a relationship. Our actions and how they are perceived result in either deposits or withdrawals being made into this account. Deposits would include little acts of kindness, general politeness and the keeping of promises – anything that increases your credibility. Criticism and disloyalty are likely to have a negative effect and result in a withdrawal. To put this into the context of leading by example, by making deposits you will build up a reserve of goodwill and trust that will enhance your credibility and the receptiveness of others. For real credibility your actions must be sincere. People will sense insincerity, often unconsciously, and the net result is uncertainty that destroys trust and depletes that bank balance.

Covey also draws our attention to the fact that we often think that the people closest to us require less regular or intense attention. In fact, the opposite can be true. The further apart we are, the more understanding people are in relation to the paucity of support we give. So, to really strengthen your emotional account with someone, you need to be making real, regular and frequent deposits. Importantly, small deposits and withdrawals set the tone of the relationship. Since big withdrawals are usually very obvious, they will tend to manifest as issues and be promptly addressed. The smaller ones often pass relatively unnoticed but, over time, the erosion of trust is significant. Even to some internal customers you may be the face of the organisation (as you represent the leadership) and repairing an excessively overdrawn account may take a lot of time and effort.

The emotional account is also a very useful driver to help embed the concept of the internal customer. It is critical that all your converts see every single person in the organisation as part of customer service because they serve someone. The better their levels of service, the more likely it is that they will have a larger account with that person. The Jenga® model is useful in helping people understand the interrelatedness of all levels of the organisation. Levels of internal customer service affect the entire organisation and impact on turnover, profitability, opportunities for promotion, job satisfaction and, eventually, even job security!

You need to *inspire people* to learn new behaviours rather than telling them what to do. Colleagues will want to work with you to solve problems and, in so doing, improve the collaborative process. Strangely, a focus on solutions is not the point: we're looking for a better process for finding solutions. This is demonstrated by the parable of the camels:

> Once upon a time, in a desert land, there was a poor father who died, leaving his three sons his eleven camels. His wishes for dividing them up caused his sons great difficulty, and almost resulted in the family being split forever.
>
> "To my eldest son, half my camels; to my middle son, one quarter of my camels; and to my youngest son, one sixth," was the instruction of the old man's will. Eleven camels cannot be divided by two, four or six, and the three sons argued back and forth for weeks over who would get what. The wives and children of the sons got involved, and all the distant relations, too.
>
> Finally, they decided to seek the assistance of the wise old woman who lived outside the village. They

explained the problem, and she thought for a long time. "This is a difficult situation," she said. "Perhaps it would help if I gave you my camel. I am too old to ride him now, so you may have him."

Bewildered, the sons took the old lady's camel. Now there were twelve camels. The eldest son took six. The middle son took three. The youngest took two. There was one camel left over. They returned it to the old lady. She simply nodded, and smiled.

To be like this wise person, you need to:

- Ask for contributions without trying to push an agenda
- Offer your thoughts and invite challenges
- Do something constructive e.g. if the cleaner is off and everyone is complaining about the overflowing wastepaper baskets, go and empty them yourself rather than telling someone else to do it!

EMPOWERMENT TO THE PEOPLE

Do you remember our point about persuading people by getting them involved? You can help this process by fostering a climate that invites engagement and offers people challenging roles. Where possible, match these opportunities to their best skills and ensure as far as possible that everyone gets an attractive role. The way you frame the job will affect effort and input. And express your appreciation of their efforts.

As trite as this may seem, never underestimate the influence you have over people just by having positive expectations of them! Enthusiastic use of this Pygmalion effect permits you to delegate tasks that are slightly beyond people's current capabilities. Then, through specific and sincere positive reinforcement, they are encouraged to succeed. Even if some are unable to sustain your levels of endurance and quit the organisation, you should see value in them so clearly that they come to see it in themselves. You might get a letter with, *I don't miss working there but I do miss working with you.*

In *The One Minute Manager*, Ken Blanchard and Spencer Johnson emphasise the importance of timely recognition, especially praise. Praise in public: this will reinforce your position as one who gives praise – who has the authority to do so – as well as the obvious benefit to the recipient. Try to do this as soon as possible after the praiseworthy event.

Delegation and empowerment are two key skills for managers wishing to maximise the performance of capable subordinates. These skills are the foundation of good supervisory leadership. By setting an example, you demonstrate your positive view of people through stretching them to reach their full potential.

There are many opportunities for coaching people. According to the Centre for Management and Organisation Effectiveness, 75% of coaching opportunities are unplanned and/or unscheduled. Examples of this include when a specific project or assignment is behind schedule; helping someone improve their levels of performance; absenteeism; instances of poor motivation; new members joining the team; conflict situations and breakdowns in communication. Look out for any of these as opportunities to get the best out of your staff.

You will need to:

- Help others to see the need for change and prepare for it
- Treat people with respect and strive to give them the best chance of success
- Help people grow through their work by giving them opportunities to develop
- Build on strengths and neutralise weaknesses
- Encourage your staff to stretch and take calculated risks
- Build commitment to common goals
- Actively look for opportunities to delegate
- Take time to define assignments clearly, taking into account the delegates' levels of competence and commitment
- Delegate with positive enthusiasm and make sure there are very clear benefits to the delegate.

Do not to fall into the boss' 'no-one can do it as well as me' trap. You should delegate tasks to people who show the appropriate levels of competence and commitment. Even outside your cause, you should encourage people to be responsible for actions and results using their own initiative and ingenuity. The goal is to create a situation where staff give their total commitment to a cause that has, in effect, also become theirs. Don't forget the recognition aspect when your staff return with a job well done. Praise them in front of their colleagues and peers, taking advantage of the moment of accomplishment to cement the lessons learned.

You should also make use of learning opportunities through a review processes – and don't forget to look for key lessons for yourself.

Before we add a few more tips to your toolbox, here's an important perspective to bear in mind: the squeaky wheel gets oiled the most. Make sure you pay attention to all the wheels in your vehicle for change, not only the ones that most demand your attention! This, of course, refers to the **training of your staff**.

You are more likely to get better results from people if your focus remains on the *task* rather than the person. While you need to understand what motivates this person in order to get the task done well, remember that the *task* is the thing you need done. Try to make this a conversation rather than a lecture. Use questions and reinforce what went well. Where possible, have more 'do more of X' statements than 'do less of Y' statements. If a staff member's head is full of what he shouldn't do, it's often difficult to translate this into what he should do. Offer a few suggestions on what could be done differently, but don't overload people. It's better to have more frequent discussions than to try to do too much at once, and these will also add to your emotional bank account with that person.

The prevailing culture in your organisation is probably not very empowering for most. Consequently, you are likely to be confronted frequently with people who are not only demotivated but also disempowered. Part of your job in selling a new direction is to help people feel, see and believe that they can make a difference. Whilst a well presented customer service perspective is likely to be motivating, you are also likely to field objections around the perceived small likelihood of success as a result of individual actions. There will be many who want to believe in your offer and to commit to it, but don't feel suitably empowered to be able to make a difference.

Covey has developed a very useful model to help people conceptualise how they can make a difference. He suggests issues being grouped in two concentric circles: the inner circle of *influence* and the outer circle of *concern* (see Figure 5).

The outer circle of concern represents the things that cause us concern but over which we believe we have no influence. The inner circle represents the things we can affect through our choices. Covey explains that we can

Fig 5: Circles of Concern & Circles of Influence

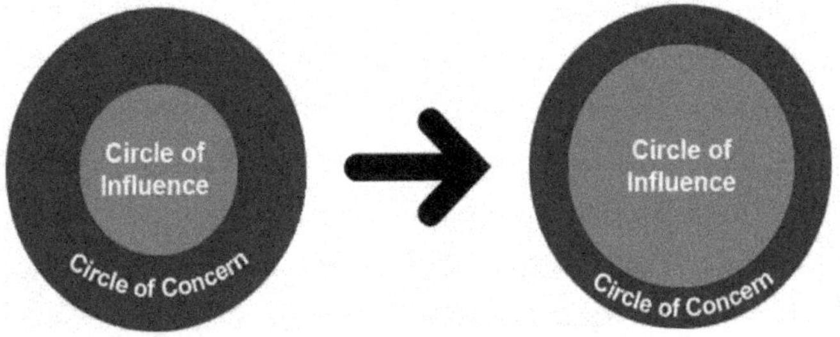

only really produce results by focusing on the inner circle. By focusing our activities and energies on the inner circle, we can cause it to grow in size and narrow a gap that previously appeared insurmountable. In some cases the narrowing will only be slight and in others it can be significant. The longer and more intensely we work on the inner circle, the more it will grow. If you share a common outer circle with others and each work on your inner circle, the effect on the gap is likely to be even more significant. If we mix our metaphors slightly, an unstable Jenga® tower will become progressively more stable as more blocks are placed where there are gaps. The more blocks are replaced, the more solid the foundation, while replacing any single block is unlikely to achieve this. Each person in the organisation effectively has a block in their hands. By working together over time, there is likely to be a significant effect.

A STITCH IN TIME

People often find it difficult to work together when overwhelmed by crises. When you are up to your neck in the mud fighting alligators, it's hard to remember that you've come to drain the swamp! You need to help people to retain their perspective, deal with the alligators and drain the swamp drop by drop, and to do all these at the same time! We believe the framework proposed by Roger Fischer and Alan Sharp in their book *Lateral Leadership* (see Figure 6) is a very useful aid.

Fig 6: A Logical Approach to Analysis & Planning

	Where we've come from	Where we're headed
Theory	**2. Analysis** Use of models, deduction, Interference, etc to try and understand the cause i.e why we are where we are	**3. Strategy and/or Planned Solutions** - Brain storming - Generate Options - Evaluate Them - Make Choices
Reality	**1. What happened** - Facts without any analytical Input - Perspectives - Mine - Theirs - The 'Objective' Perspective	**4. Implementation of Plan** N.B Details is important i.e. who, what, where, when & now

By adapting your leadership and management style, you will make your staff and the boss more likely to accept what you are offering. The techniques we have listed are all highly effective, but the process will take time and may suffer setbacks. Don't fight any single point too hard – if you're advancing on a number of fronts, the occasional reversal on any specific issue is easier to accept.

Jo sighs. "I guess that I can see some progress, and I can see that there's been some gradual increase in the rate of change of the whole project. I definitely need to work less hard than I did before to get similar results."

"Exactly!" Jerry is delighted. "Where you had to plan every step and every word at the beginning, you're now able to make things happen in the right way with far less effort. That's the tipping point in action. Really, all that remains is for it to become self-sustaining so that your input can change from getting the wheels of change turning to making sure that nothing interferes with the ongoing process of change – keeping the wheels oiled, I guess."

Jo is hurt. "But all this is because of my work. Surely they couldn't carry on without me?"

Jerry smiles. "Jo," he says, "one of the hardest things for a manager is letting go. That's exactly what Brian struggles with. But if you have taken your team along this journey and truly empowered them, then of course they don't need you there, holding their hands. They can manage this without you."

There's a benefit to a gradually increasing rate of change that Jo and Jerry may have overlooked. At first, the slow rate of change may be frustrating, but it gives you time to practise your skills and become a better and more responsive manager. You get used to change taking place and driving it forward. You can make mistakes and still have time to put them right.

With time, you get better and better at the process of change at the same time that change is speeding up around you. By the time you hit the log phase of our bacterial growth diagram, you need to be an expert at managing the process. Any mistakes here could have such rapid consequences that you have little or no time to correct them.

Just as we saw with the golf ball's flight being hugely affected by tiny changes in the grip of the golf club, so the scope for disaster increases rapidly and exponentially as the rate of change increases. It's just as well you have time to practise: you wouldn't want to be the one changing the wheels of the Formula One racing car without having had time to practise!

> Jo is convinced – in part. "Jerry," she murmurs, "what if it actually doesn't happen? What if nothing actually happens? What if we're constantly and endlessly getting closer and closer, and never actually get there?"

What, indeed? Is it all a waste of time? All the effort you've put in: understanding your boss, understanding yourself and understanding your organisation, finding and developing allies, empowering your team and coaching them, will this all have been for nothing?

Happily, the answer is "No!" Let's explore this in Chapter 13.

WHAT'S IN IT FOR YOU?

THE CRUNCHY BIT

It's possible that a tipping point could be reached between you and your boss where his initial resistance to your ideas suddenly starts to lessen. If you can get him to buy in to the process wholeheartedly, that would be enormously helpful to you. There's most definitely a chance that any approach to him for assistance before you reach this tipping point could blow up in your face. Make sure you pick the right moment! The benefits are potentially great, however, so it's worth considering actively but carefully.

The thrust of the book has been organisational change. But organisations are made up of people, and you are one of those people. The skills you've learnt as you've read through the text are applicable in your current job, but could just as easily be applied to another work setting or in your home life.

Adhering to the processes, techniques and principles we've outlined will enhance your chances of success with the project. What you'll get out of it as a person and a manager, however, is not entirely tied to the success of effecting the change you're after. You will derive many benefits whether this project succeeds or fails.

Whether you decide to stay in your organisation or leave, your learning from the process will stand you in good stead. Through your enhanced abilities, your value to other organisations will

increase and you will have grown as a person, team member,
manager and leader.

Good luck, and good hunting!

SHOWING YOUR HAND

We have written this book to assist you in recognising your situation and doing something about it. We've outlined conventional management wisdom in relation to these common issues and have gone into some detail about possible solutions. This approach is designed to present your boss with a mirror on his behaviour and how it impacts on his team and on the organisation. We've advised that you don't disclose too much detail too early in the process. For every rule, however, there are exceptions. There is a scenario to consider that, whilst risky, can have immense potential benefit…

Consider this: if you were a power-hungry and control-focused boss, would you not be interested in the tactics and plans that a potential adversary may intend to use against you? And, if that information showed how you could improve things so that you not only had control over people's actions but their hearts and minds, and could also achieve improved levels of productivity and profitability, would you choose to ignore it? If your boss could choose between doing these things himself or having someone else do them and embarrassing him, which would he choose?

We have deliberately left this suggestion until the end

of the book because we realise that your boss has probably previously been exposed to data, arguments and facts that suggest that his approach is inappropriate. He's probably been immune to this evidence because he regards himself as the only expert on his particular company, in his particular field, at this particular time. There is no identical comparator; so all comparisons are worthless!

You may have seen the futility of trying to change his mind. But remember the power of context: Gladwell cites numerous compelling examples of how critical context is in determining how we perceive, integrate and process information. Finding an adversary's battle plans lying on the floor is a chance for an advantage that no military general would pass up. **What if your boss was to find this book conspicuously on the staff room table, your desk or elsewhere after a debate with you?** If he's started to realise that you have ideas and plans that are intriguing but uncomfortable to him, would he not want to know where those ideas had come from?

If you do choose to leave this book for your boss to find, it first requires a careful assessment of how far down the road of change he has gone. As a general rule, we suggest using his openness to the concept of a business plan as a yardstick of how far he has travelled.

We have previously warned that a business plan may be one of the last things you will be able to address directly. If you feel he is now fairly open to this idea (not necessarily an advocate, perhaps, but giving even grudging consideration), the time may be right to leave a copy of this book somewhere he's likely to find it.

One small proviso: you may have a very transactional boss who very closely examines accounts and loves numbers. These bosses may not need much convincing in relation to a business plan, but don't necessarily fully appreciate the value of human capital. In these cases, the business plan is not your indicator of how beneficial it might be to leave a copy of this book prominently displayed on your desk. Here, the internal customer and customer service agenda needs to have been implemented before you can consider revealing your agenda.

Make sure you assess the stress your boss is under. As we've seen, when under pressure he will revert to his default personality type and is then unlikely to be open to anything controversial. On the other hand, with the right timing and context, he will probably pick up the book and read it closely. If he decides to adopt some, most, or all of what we have presented here, your mission is complete! With a bit of luck, you may have also found your boss is now your powerful ally, or perhaps just less resistant to your ideas than before.

WHAT'S IN IT FOR YOU?

Sir George Russell CBE in reviewing this book said, "After your first week in a new job, you sit with your colleagues and say '*If only they would listen*'. With a bit of luck, one day you will be one of 'them'. This book gives you an outline on how to be a good one of them."

We certainly agree about being a 'good one of them'.

Jo's worried. "What if the plan doesn't work? I'll have wasted all my time and effort to get nothing. Absolutely nothing. Except stress and ulcers!"

Our advice to her (and to you!) serves as a fitting conclusion to this book:

Managing processes like this, even with a formal mandate, is very challenging – particularly within an adversarial or patriarchal culture. It's by applying the processes you've learnt through this book that immense informal growth and development opportunities arise for you.

Most managers are given support after promotion or in anticipation of promotion. These managers are likely to have some form of positional power. You may have a similar status, or you may have decided to redefine an organisational ethos from the bottom-up – with nothing other than attitude, enthusiasm, motivation, tenacity, a plan and some complementary sets of skills!

During this period you've been honing your ability to persuade, motivate and negotiate, often from a position of reduced power. Not only this, but you've improved your ability to be effective, influential and assertive. You've gained insight and experience in understanding how different people relate to one another. You've had opportunities to build, lead and motivate teams by taking advantage of group dynamics and staff desires. You've been able to engineer your very own tipping point!

You've also had the opportunity to develop a comprehensive set of skills for the future. This can all make you a far more competent senior manager. After all, if your boss showed all these traits, you would probably be quite happy with your lot and not trying to make changes.

It's important always to work on self-improvement. You need to grow as a person and a manager. While everything you do should support your goal, just as importantly, it should support you! Please see Appendix A for a short list of resources that might be useful to you in your ongoing development.

If the whole process fails after you've committed significant effort and time, you could easily get a job in an even more senior position using the skills, techniques and principles you have learned and perfected.

On the other hand... If the plan succeeds, will you want some form of recognition and promotion? Or will you be happy in a less powerful position than your boss?

There is no doubt that the better you become at the skills and processes we've discussed, the better prepared you'll be to be a good boss. So promotion opportunities are likely.

There are lots of positives that come with promotion, but these usually also come at a price – work-life balance being among the most frequent casualties. Depending on what motivates and drives you, you could use your position of influence to your advantage, and get satisfaction from that without having a title to prove how important you are. This could give you more time to focus on other important things in your life.

At the start of this book, Jo asked, "Should I stay or should I go?" Now she has choices – as do you! Choices to stay or to go, and choices she can make from a position of strength. That position of strength comes from what you now have to offer: greater experience, greater expertise in managing difficult circumstances and motivating people in spite of that, and greater confidence in your own ability.

The interview process, as you know, often depends less on your CV and previous job titles and more on your ability to tell stories of how you've handled situations and what you've done in the face of adversity. No matter what the outcome is where you are now – and we hope it really does work out well for you and are confident that it can – you'll be in a much better place to find the position that suits **you** in the future.

Good luck!

APPENDIX A: Your Ongoing Development

It's all very well supporting others, but don't overlook your own development needs. We have, in the book, referred to a number of courses and books we feel will significantly help you to move towards your goal. An added bonus is that these skills are not only useful in our context, their acquisition will also yield useful tips, techniques and other information that you can apply in many other management settings. So, should you choose to leave your current job, you will not only have some interesting experience but will also have learned some additional skills.

Some courses and books we highly recommend are:

- **What got you here won't get you there: How successful people become even more successful,** *Goldsmith & Reiter*
- **The coach: creating partnerships for a competitive edge,** *Stowell & Starcevich*
- **Good to Great.** *Jim Collins*
- **The 7 Habits of Highly Effective People,** *Stephen Covey*
  This is available in a number of formats, including book, audiobook and seminar. If you can make it to a seminar, you won't regret it!

- **Assertiveness Training,** *Excel Communications*
- **Face-to-Face Selling,** *The Forum Corporation*
  While run-of-the mill sales training programmes tend not to focus on the relationship selling issues we have outlined in this book, the *Face-to-Face Selling* programme does this exceptionally well.
- **Situational Leadership II,** *Ken Blanchard*
  The concepts presented in this course are relatively simple but we would strongly recommend you attend a Situational Leadership II training course.
- **Getting to Yes,** *Fisher & Ury*
- **Wilson Learning's Social Styles Training,**
  This course will help increase your ability to work more effectively with others, even when they are stressed.
- **Nudge,** *Thaler & Sunstein*
- **Lateral Leadership,** *Fischer & Sharpe*
- **Management Learning & Coaching Ltd's** online academy (http://www.management-learning.co.uk/)
- **The Tipping Point,** *Malcolm Gladwell*

REFERENCES &
CONTACT DETAILS

Advanced Institute of Management Research (2014) Our research. [Accessed 10 October 2014] http://www.aimresearch.org/our-research

Amazon (2014) Amazon Mission Statement [Accessed 10 October 2014] http://www.amazon.com/Careers-Homepage/b?ie=UTF8&node=239364011

Blanchard, K H & Johnson, S (1982). *The one minute manager*. New York: Morrow

Cameron, K S & Quinn, R E (1999). *Diagnosing and changing organizational culture: Based on the competing values framework*. Reading, MA: Addison-Wesley.

Collins, J (2001) *Good to great – why some companies make the leap... and others don't*. New York: Harper Collins

Covey, S R (2013) *The 7 habits of highly effective people: powerful lessons in personal change*. New York: Simon & Schuster

Ebrahim, G J & Ranken, J P (1988) *Primary healthcare: reorienting organisational support*. Macmillan.

Fine, C (2006) *A Mind of Its Own: How Your Brain Distorts and Deceives*. New York: Norton

Fisher, R & Sharp, A (2004) *Lateral Leadership: Getting It Done When You Are Not The Boss.* London: Profile Books

Fisher, R & Ury, W (1981) *Getting to Yes: Negotiating Agreement Without Giving In.* New York: Penguin

Forum Corporation (2014) *Improving sales effectiveness.* [Accessed 10 October 2014] http://www.forum.com/business-challenges/improving-sales-effectiveness/

Gladwell, M (2000). *The tipping point: How little things can make a big difference.* Boston: Little, Brown

Gladwell, M (2008). *Outliers: the story of success.* New York: Little, Brown

Goldsmith, M & Reiter, M (2007). *What got you here won't get you there: How successful people become even more successful.* New York, NY: Hyperion

Management Learning and Coaching (2014) *Online academy.* [Accessed 10 October, 2014] http://www.management-learning.co.uk/

Priestley, D (2010) *Become a Key Person of Influence: The 5 Step Sequence to becoming one of the most highly valued and highly paid people in your industry.* St. Albans, Ecademy Press

Schneider, W E (2000) Why good management ideas fail: the neglected power of organizational culture. *Strategy & Leadership*, Vol. 28:1, pp.24 – 29

Stowell, S J & Starcevich, M M (2008) *The coach: creating partnerships for a competitive edge.* Salt Lake City, Utah: Center for Management and Organization Effectiveness.

Thaler, R H & Sunstein, C R (2009). *Nudge: improving decisions about health, wealth, and happiness.* New York: Penguin Books